Pigeon

The Early Years

Featuring Articles Originally Published in:
The Pigeon Progress Advance

Florence Gwinn Schluchter
Author of some of these newspaper articles

Duane Wurst
Editor and Graphic Artist

ISBN-13: 978-1544987965
ISBN-10: 154498796X

Text and cover design by Duane Wurst, Berne Studio
Cover images © Duane Wurst

Images were provided by The Pigeon Historical Society Museum
Archives, and are protected by copyright.

A special thank you to The Pigeon Progress
for the use of these articles, and to their contributors and reporters. who
provided the Pigeon Progress-Advance with their historic knowledge.

Printed in the United States of America

Dedicated To The Memory of Florence Gwinn Schlucter

Florence was an active member of The Pigeon Historical Society and
without her work this book would not have been possible.
She was born November 19, 1889, in Caseville, Michigan, and married
Alvin G. Schluchter. In 1985 Florence passed, leaving us with her written
memories and a love for the history of our area.

Forward

Pigeon is very lucky to have had a newspaper published throughout out its history. The Pigeon Historical Society and Depot Museum have copies of most of these newspapers, both physical and on microfilm. Using these sources this book will discuss the early history of Pigeon.

Florence Gwinn Schluchter was an active member of the Pigeon Historical Society until her death. She was also an author and wrote her autobiography and a book on the History of Hayes Methodist Church. In 1977 the Pigeon Progress asked her to write a weekly column on the history of Pigeon. We have included many of the articles she wrote for the newspaper in this book. We also have included other articles that were published throughout the years, in an attempt to present a balanced look at the early history of Pigeon.

This book is in no way a complete history of the area. Instead, it is a slice of history as presented through the years in the Pigeon Progress-Advance newspapers.

As you read, remember that these articles were written in the 1890s though the 1970s. When the writer talks about the location of businesses, they are talking about it's location then, when the article was written. This can become confusing, but if you realize the year it was written, it will become less so.

Editor

DuaneWurst

Pigeon
The Early Years

Edited by, Duane Wurst

The Primeval Region

Florence Gwinn Schluchter

From The Pigeon Progress

Because of its location, Pigeon was not settled as soon as Caseville or Bay Port. Naturally, the first explorers followed the shore of Saginaw Bay.

Only Indians enjoyed the beauty of the primeval forests. They too paddled their canoes along the shore and up the rivers. One of the Indian camps was on the east bank of the Pigeon River on the now Bruce Leipprandt farm. About one-half mile north, also on the east side of the river, one of the Indians had been buried. Each spring an Indian visited the grave. He always stopped for something to eat at the C. F. Leipprandt home.

Florence McKinnon (Morse) Gwinn, in her Pioneer History of Huron County, Michigan, 1922, wrote a description of this section of Michigan, which I will include in this history.

"Before the white man took possession of this section, great stands of white pine covered the larger portion of what is now Huron County."

"There were about 80 varieties of trees, native to Michigan and a large majority of these were found in Huron County. There were white and Norway pine, spruce, cedar, balsam, hard and soft maple, smooth and shag-bark hickory, tamarack, birch, hemlock and numerous other kinds of cone-bearing evergreen trees as well as various trees that shed their leaves in the fall."

"Besides these forests, there were in many places great stretches

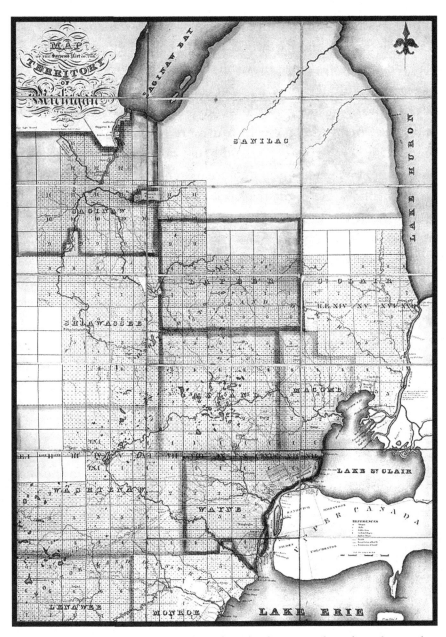

The above map, *From Wikipedia, the free encyclopedia,* shows the thumb area of Michigan as it was known in 1825. Huron County was a part of Sanilac County and had not yet been surveyed.

of marshes and swamps with a dense growth of cedar and tamarack. As a rule the oak and hardwood were to be found upon the heavy clay soil, on the swampy sandy soil the pine, hemlock and groves of oak grew. Beautiful shrubs, many of which have almost disappeared, covered the open spaces in the woods. Along the shores of the Bay and rivers, many kinds of wild fruit were growing, such as plums, grapes, wild crab apples, red and black raspberries, strawberries, and on the sand plains an abundance of huckleberries. To add to the beauty of the scene in many places, were the wild flowers, each in their season. The violets, trilliums, honeysuckle, lady slippers, wild roses and trailing arbutus."

"The bay teamed with fish. In the woods roamed the moose, deer, elk, bear, wolf, and lynx. Along the river were beaver, otter, muskrat and mink. In a spring morning the woods resounded with the music of birds."

She was well qualified to write the above description as her father, Robert Morse, Sr., settled in the Mud Creek community in 1863, when she was just five years old. Then, too, my father, Richard Gwinn Jr., was only four when his father, Richard Gwinn Sr., settled in the Hayes Community.

What wonderful times mother and father had recalling the early history of the county during the years of 1921-1922, when she was writing her book. They really loved the forests and instilled into their children the love of the woods. When I was a child, woods were still abundant. As I read her list of wild flowers, I realized she had omitted the hepaticas. They were quite rare but we did have a few under the beech tree beside the cow path and east of our creek. The other place I used to hunt for them was in Anderson's woods, across from the C. F. Leipprandt home, near the south bank of the little creek. It was my favorite spot in the woods. It had a few cedar trees, some pretty green moss, little red berries and the hepaticas as well as violets and other flowers.

In the spring, I would leave early to walk to school so I could pick flowers on the way. Great patches of adder-tongues and lilies, as we called them, grew in those woods. What if we missed and stepped in water over our rubbers, or maybe slipped off a log we had to walk on to reach a spot where especially large trilliums grew, and got both feet wet? We really didn't mind, for you had beautiful bouquets to take to the teacher who always had a few containers for them, even if not beautiful vases.

Something that most children of today are denied is the hunting of arbutus along the sand-ridge. How I loved those dainty pink flowers with their exquisite fragrance.

Five Factors

There were perhaps five (5) main factors that led to the settlement and growth of the village of Pigeon. First, as already stated, the Pigeon River; second, the lumber industry; third, the Ora Labora Colony and fourth, the railroads. The fifth reason was fertile farm land. Taking them in turn, trappers and shingle weavers were the first to arrive, they settled in Caseville which is at the mouth of the Pigeon River. Ruben Dodge and his family were the first white settlers in 1836. Mrs. Mose Gregory was his daughter. Next came Charles Smith, a land broker and hunter. He pre-empted part of the land, which now belongs to Allan Gwinn, and also part of the land which is owned by C. F. Leipprandt and sons.

In 1841 Leonard Case purchased 20,000 acres of pine land along the river. Later, in 1856, he sold his property to Francis Crawford and Mr. Martin who later sold his interest to Crawford.

Also, in 1851, Bill Handy settled on 80 acres on the Pigeon River north of the Filion Road and east of Sturm Road. (*Pigeon Progress -Advance 05-26-1977)*

A short time later Arthur McAulay purchased the now H. F. Leipprandt land from Smith and built a log home on the river bank. Canoes on the river were the means of transportation for the Handys and McAulays, as there were no roads.

"My father often related an incident regarding Mr. Handy. It happened during the time of the Civil War. He deserted from the Army and came home. One day two men stopped at Grandma Gwinn's and inquired the way to Mr. Handy's. She realized at once that they were Government men and also realized at the same time the penalty Mr. Handy would have to pay for desertion from the Army if caught. She directed the men back Grandpa's lane to the River road and on up that road to Handy's. As soon as they were gone she sent William and Richard Jr. running up the new (Sturm) road, which was shorter, to warn Handys that the men were coming."

"Mr. Handy was out in the woods, so Mrs. Handy immediately gathered all the white clothes she could find and hung them on the bushes, which, grew near the house, on the river bank. When she had finished, she said, "There, Bill will not come home." She was right. The men finally left without him.'"

"Later, however, he was caught. When they inquired as to why he had deserted, he told them it was because he got lonesome for his wife. When they learned that he had walked the entire distance from the South through woods, mostly at nights, and had lived on the game he shot, they decided that he was too good of a man to shoot. They put him back into the Army as a sharpshooter. He served in that capacity until the end of the war." "Hayes School by F. M.G. S."

Lumbering

Two large lumber camps used to operate along the Pigeon River. Namely, Francis Crawford's and Captain Water's camps. In order to reach these   camps a road was cut along the river. Pioneers used this road to reach their property. Little by little the settlers moved up the river. In 1871, Mose Gregory had charge of Crawford's camps about 12 miles (using the river road) from Caseville. Mrs. Gregory was cook. Besides the men, she had her family to cook for, making a total of 40 people.

In the early years, during the summer, the Pigeon River dried up,

Above: Francis Crawford's Home on the Pigeon River in Caseville. Below: Workers at one of the Logging Camps along Pigeon River.

to quite an extent. There was water only in the deep holes. Then in the fall the springs, at its source, would begin to flow again and little by little the fresh clear water would slowly make its way down the river. We were always interested in watching it come.

The summer and fall of 1871 had been very dry. The "Fire of 1871" broke out and was headed for Gregory's camp. They hurriedly loaded their wagons (about 8 or 10 of them) with all their belongings and hitched up their teams. (Part may have been oxen as oxen were used to a large extent in the early days. In fact, as late as 1884 the Gwinns hired Mike Conaton and his ox team for two days to assist in hauling pine logs to Cleavers Mill). Since the river bed was comparatively dry they decided that it would be the best and safest way to travel. They wet blankets in a deep hole, covered people, teams and belongings with them and started tor Caseville. At each deep hole they re-wet the blankets while sparks flew over their heads. After three fearful days they finally reached safety in Caseville, which escaped the fire. (Told to me by Lyman Gregory).

The River Drives

After the pine trees were cut, the logs were skidded out to the river and piled along the bank. Each log was marked by the initials of its owner. The logs waited at the bank for the spring flood, which would supply enough water to float the logs down the river to its mouth, where the sawmills were located. It was an exciting time when the logs were all finally in the river and the River Drivers started the drive. A jam was a thing that all the drivers dreaded. One of the worst places was a short distance south of the Filion Road. Here the river makes a sharp turn. It was called "The Devil's Elbow" by the drivers.

The log crop for Huron County in 1873 was 80,000,000 feet according to statistics in Pioneer History of Michigan, 1922.

Pioneers also logged when clearing their land. One day while visiting with our neighbor, Joe Schubach; he related one of his experiences as a young man. His father, D. Schubach was cutting logs and clearing his land. They were hauling the logs to the river so they could be taken to the sawmill.

His father evidently did not have a clock, but each morning he awakened his sons early so they could feed the team, eat their breakfast and when daylight came they could begin their work.

This particular morning when they finished breakfast it was still dark, but they decided to start work anyway, as it soon would be light from the morning sun. They loaded at load of logs, and still no daylight. They drew it to the river, and still no daylight. There was still no daylight when they loaded the second load, but as they reached the river with this second load the first rays of the sun could be seen. They had done almost a regular mornings work before the sun had even come up. Joe ended his story by saying, "That night's sleep was short!"

Newcomers

By 1860, other people began to settle in what is now Hayes Community. Five Anderson men, Richard Gwinn Sr. and Charles Stewart.

When the Hayes School District was organized in 1862, the names of William Horn Sr., John Herbert, George Wilfong, Solomon Barr, Henry Newman and John Simpson were on the list of families at the Hayes community. *(Pigeon Progress-Advance 06-03-1977)*

The Roads

The Sand Road was the first cut through the wilderness. It was the main road for several years, and was used by the stagecoach, which went from Port Austin to Saginaw. People in the early days had to go to Saginaw for any business regarding their land.

The Sand Road, as I remember it as a child, when we went to Grandpa Morses every Sunday for dinner; before attending Sunday school and church in the afternoon at the Hayes M.E. church, was for one-way traffic only.

If someone met another person, you had to start looking for some place between the trees and stumps that lined the track to pull to one side so the other person could pass. It did not happen very often as traffic was very light.

By 1860, the Sturm Road had been cut south as far as the Limerick Road. Then it traveled east to the river, where it joined the log road, which went south along' the river. Mother often entertained us children by telling us about things that happened when she was a child. They lived on the Sand Road. People who lived farther east used Grandpa's lane to reach their trail to their homes. The lane went past their log house across the bridge, over the small creek to the log barn and barnyard. Mr. Bill, whom they called Dutch Billy, as well as others often failed to close the barnyard gate after they had gone through. The children would have to run and shut the gate, this was a chore that they did not care for.

Hardships Of Newcomers

**George and Ella Newman
Henry Newman's Son**

Many were the hardships of those early settlers. For instance the Henry Newman family had very hard times. To make matters worse, Mr. Newman died leaving Mrs. Newman with 'several small children. She found work for awhile in the Crawford Boarding House, for his "Lumber Jacks" in Caseville.

George and Ella Newman . .

Besides her small wages she was allowed any left overs at the end of the day to carry home to her children. It would often be after dark before she 'could leave for home. The Sturm Road was cut out as far as the Filion Road. From there she would follow the River Road. About the time she should be coming the oldest child would light a pine and hold it up so she could see the flame and know where to turn off the River Road and follow the trail through what is now the Riverside Nursery to her log home just west of the Railroad. At one time, someone asked Mrs. Newman if she were not afraid to walk up that road through the woods after dark. She replied "No! Mr. Newman walks with me! "

Many times there was nothing to eat in the house; I recall Mr. George Newman Sr. saying, "All we had to eat was a few rutabagas in the garden. These we ate raw.

He also told Isabel Newman that one time when the only thing in the house was a bar of soap. He looked at it and wondered if by any chance he might be able to eat it since he was so hungry!

Ora Labora Colony Drawing depicting the colony

Ora Labora Colony

The Colony purchased many acres of land from the Government in 1857-1858. They established a town between Caseville and Wild Fowl Bay (Old Bay Port). Each settler held a piece of land in his own right. Later, fever, ague and other illness took their toll, plus the fact that several of the men were drafted for the Civil War. This left only the older men and women to carry on the work. This made the load too heavy to bear, so the Colony was disbanded in 1871..

The case was presented to the Legislature and homesteads were granted them by the State under proper restrictions. Their land, to a great extent, bordered the Pigeon River and that section became known as "The German Settlement." They soon built a log church on the east bank of the river one-half mile south of the Pigeon River bridge on M-142, west of Pigeon. They allowed the building to be used as a school. *(Pigeon Progress-Advance 06-09-1977)*

The first teacher was Herman Rodel (he might have taught in the Colony). He was followed by Frances Snell of Bay Port and she was followed by Florence Morse of Mud Creek (Later, Mrs. Richard Gwinn, Jr.) She taught two terms and then again from the years 1880 to 1882.

The names of the families whose children attended school included Heinerman, Muentener, Maier, Robitski, Johnson, Ebert, Eimers, Moeller, Dietzel, J Schledjeski and Wasserman.

(Taken from mother's class book.)

The last year she taught, the school district bought the church as the congregation had purchased 20 acres for $1.00 on the northwest corner of North Caseville and Berne roads. They built a frame church on that property. The school term was for five months of the year. There were no uniform books. Instead pupils brought all kinds of books and parents could not understand why these were not all right. Mother boarded with the Frobes, she had worked for them when she was a gal, when the Frobes lived in the Colony, Mother wrote the following in her *Pioneer History of Huron County*:

Brown-Hyser Wedding

Among the interesting events of that time was the wedding of Alice Hyser and William Brown on New Years Day in 1877. Miss Morse and the Froebe family, attended this ceremony. It took place at the old Hyser farm, a few miles up the river from where Pigeon is now situated. The lumber road followed the bank of the river, through the woods, (if it could be called a road). The whole party rode in a wagon with boards on instead of a box and once this vehicle got tangled up with the numerous logs that projected into the highway. Everyone had to help get the logs out of the track.

On arriving at the Hyser home which was, of course, a big building forming an L shaped structure, they found that all of the other guests were there. For seats there were benches around the room and in the center a bench on which sat the bride, groom, bridesmaid and best man. Everyone had a splendid chance to see the bride's dress, which was made of a pretty blue material.

At one end of the same room was the long table already spread for the dinner. O. P. Chapin was the officiating Justice of Peace. He must have had the dinner in view for the marriage ceremony only lasted about one minute. There was but scant attention paid to the congratulations but rather the guests congratulated themselves on the abundance of good things provided. Plenty of roast goose, honey, pies, cakes, and other dainties. A dinner like this was a rare treat in those days and nearly every housewife within reach had assisted in its preparation. When it was over it was time to go home, for people did not travel in autos in that day.

Mud Creek

Mother taught again in the Mud Creek School. She used the same class book. The children who attended in 1882 and 1883 gives us the names of most of the families who had established homes and cleared at least part of their farms. They are as follows: Louise Harder, John and Alfred Morse, Edwin and Willie Gardner, J, Hugh, James and Charles Smith, Walter, Lydia and Lucinda Douker, John, James, "Ton", Willie, Agnes, and Mary Richmond, Eliza Danks, Rachael Douker, Martin Cornell, Ephraim Brechtel and Louis Davis.

On the next page, I found a few more names. These people attended the school the next year. They were Edna Gardner, John Herbert, Annie Davis, Ella Verbeck and Mary Wideman.

Sturm Family

The August Sturm family lived in Cincinnati, Ohio. Then came the Civil War, in which Mr. Sturm served. When the war was over they moved to Saginaw, Michigan. Here Martin and Rosa were born. Mr. Sturm found work in the lumber industry.

They had friends who had lived in the Ora Labora Colony who told them about land in Huron County, which could be bought reasonably after it had been lumbered. So they decided to move into the new country. They bought land on the southeast corner of what, is now Sturm and Campbell Roads, in 1871. At first they lived in one of the houses in the Colony, which had been made vacant by the colony being disbanded.

They worked hard clearing a spot for a shanty and also a garden. Soon they built a log cabin, where their last child. Edward (Big Ed) was born.

A clipping "Martin Sturm tells of Pioneer Days," states:

"Father Sturm had erected a shanty 12 X 14 ft. on his new land. A man from Sebewaing with a team of mules moved us to the new property. A bad snow storm prevented him from returning to Sebewaing and the only shelter for the family, the teamster and mules was the little shanty. There we all huddled and I never slept a wink all night." *(Pigeon Progress-Advance 06-23-1977)*

August Sturm

A chimney sweep from Hanover, Germany, set down the roots of the Sturm family in the Thumb of Michigan. How he happened to get to America is an amusing story which has been preserved by his granddaughter, Lillian Sturm Leipprandt. Her grandfather, August Mueller, was born in 1828, and in the course of his adventurous and colorful life, changed his name, his homeland and his fortune.

He was determined to come to America, and dreamed about his ambition while sweeping chimneys. His job eventually involved him in a romantic adventure and provided him with the money he needed for the ocean passage.

A young lover, whose lady had been whisked away to a convent by her parents, offered Mueller enough money for the ship to America if he could spirit her out of the convent. He started immediately to clean the chimneys at the convent, while discretely locating the quarters

16

August Sturm   Mrs. Sturm

the young lady occupied. He found her grieving for her young man and eager to be reunited.

His last day's work at the convent had arrived, and as usual, he came with a big black bag on his back, filled with the brushes of his trade. When he left in the evening, the young lady was in the bag when he slung it over his shoulder.

But the plan almost failed. Before reaching the exit, Mueller was stopped by a sister. He stood quietly, and the girl in the bag hardly dared to breathe. But the pause was only momentary for the sister suspected nothing, and only inquired of the sweep's well being.

Mueller saw the lovers reunited, and left the same night for his long journey. To avoid any possible trouble with the authorities over the matter, he changed his name to August Sturm. He found his way to Cincinnati and in 1854, married Marie Eckelkamp.

In 1871 the fire swept through Huron County. The news was taken to Father by Mrs. Henry Moeller, Sr. He came to Sebewaing by boat. He walked to Kilmanagh, where he was told it was impossible to get through. He continued, however, and after being lost for a time he reached the Pigeon River two miles south of Pigeon. By following the river he reached the Mathias Notter farm and from there reached home at 2:00 a.m.

In 1873 my father worked in the woods between Pigeon and Elkton. He came home one Saturday night and found we had nothing to eat. My parents were praying people and trusted the Lord would find a way to help. Sunday morning Henry and I went to the road and found flour on the snow. The Glosser boys had gone to Caseville with a grist and coming home in the evening the bag opened right at our gate and spilled the whole bag of middling on the snow. We picked it up and lived on that middling for two weeks.

That log cabin stood for a great many years, just back of the present house now owned by DeVere Sturm.

Mr. Sturm had to return to Saginaw to earn money to pay for the land and keep the family. Maria and the five children were left alone while August went to work.

Their neighbors were the Hoveners. They lived on the northeast corner of the Sturm and Campbell Road (Mr. Hovener later taught at the Turner and Hayes Schools).

The summer and fall of 1871 were very dry! The fire of 1871 broke out. It was rapidly coming in the direction of the Sturm home, and Mrs. Sturm did not know what to do. The neighbors told her to carry her belongings and furniture to the garden hoping the fire would not burn them there.

Suddenly the wind changed. It took the fire in another direction. This saved the house but it burned the belongings and furniture.

Before the wind changed the smoke was so thick that they could hardly breathe, so she had the children lie on the ground around the dug well with their faces toward the water. She had to hold the younger ones so they would not fall into the well. (The baby was just two weeks old). By doing so they survived.

Trying times followed. Many and many a night the children went to bed crying from hunger, since they had no food.

The next summer, Martin and Rosa, barefooted, picked raspberries and blackberries in the woods. They carried the berries down the trail to Caseville and sold them for $.05 a quart. That is if they could make the sale.

The only book in the house was a German Bible. Mrs. Sturm read it to the children, faithfully. Since there was no school she taught them to read using the Bible as her textbook.

Very hard circumstances continued until 1875. Sophia married

Simon Wilfong. The wedding was held in the Wilfong home. They were married by C. F. Leipprandt. hand-made wedding certificate of ordinary tablet paper was made by Henry Muentener, who was a beautiful writer. He also embellished it with fancy designs. The certificate is owned by Lillian Leipprandt. Martin Sturm said he never had seen so much food as they had for the wedding. *(Pigeon Progress-Advance 06-30-1977)*

From then on Sophia shared with her family when they were in need of food. Martin also told that on Sunday morning they were dressed for church, then he would walk in the garden until he heard singing down the trail through the woods to the north. Soon, C. F. Leipprandt and two Steinman men would emerge. The mosquitoes were also singing so the men wore nets over their heads and carried branches from trees in their hands to brush off the mosquitoes.

The Sturms would join them and all walk to the German Methodist church on the river bank just south of M-142. Little by little the land was cleared, crops sown, gardens planted. They also had a nice vineyard, which was north of the log house.

Rumor had it that Mr. Sturm kept a loaded gun behind the kitchen door. It also said that he would use it on anyone who was caught stealing his grapes. The rumor of the loaded gun was correct. He would give his grandchildren peppermints and warn them not to touch the loaded gun. It was his army musket.

A loaded gun in the early days was a common thing, as it took quite some time to load them and they really had no place to hang them. At first, Fathers gun stood behind the door but later it was hung on a rack in the shed. If he had been hunting and did not shoot at game, the gun was left loaded. I've often watched father load his old musket. It was quite a task!

Today, the August Sturm farm is owned by his great grandson, DeVere Sturm, and the road in front of the property bears the Sturm name.

I have written about three of the families who settled not far from

Pigeon. One in 1861 or 1862, one in 1871 and one in 1883. Their experiences could be duplicated many times by other families. What an interesting history it would make if the experiences of the various families could be recorded.

Yackle

The family . name in Germany was spelled Yakle but was changed to Yackle after they arrived in America.

John George Yackle left his old home in Weiler 24 Hote Wurtenberg Germany in 1882 to come to America. The home was in the foothills of the Black Forest.

He came to Unionville, where he worked in a Stave mill.

Christina, the mother, and her nine children joined the father in Unionville in 1883.

On the train from New York City, she found no one who could speak German until she reached Akron, Mich. when a Mrs. Huntsberger boarded the train. She was the Post Mistress of Akron. Mrs. Huntsberger was the grandmother of Frances Anklam Buerker. She later became the Pigeon post mistress. .

Mr. Yackle met the train in Unionville, took his family to the hotel for supper before he took them 2 1/2 miles east of town. Here he had built a small shanty in the woods. While living there a bear came one night and prowled around their shanty.

ln 1884, Mr. Yackle heard of land for sale near Berne. "He went to Berne and purchased 40 acres of land just east of the present. town of Pigeon. "The Fire of 1881 had burned over part of the land, which was mostly woods and swamp. His friend, George Mast, whom he had known in Germany, kept the Yackle family in his home, near Sebewaing, until Mr. Yackle could get a shanty built on his property.

Their tenth child, Frieda (Mrs, Russel Murdoch) was born in that shanty. Later, a frame house was built.

The land was finally cleared by hand labor only. The family with the help of a team of oxen did the hard work. Those first years were very hard, as they were for most of the pioneers in the area.

While in Unionville they became acquainted with a lady who had brown Bantam chickens. Yackles wanted some too. Gottlieb, their 11 or 12 year old child, walked to Unionville one day and returned the next carrying a pail with a dozen eggs in one hand and a 'setting hen' under the other arm. There was no building in which to 'set the hen' so they fixed a nest in the corner of the shanty.

I do not, know where they kept the little chickens when they hatched, but in the early and even later days it was customary to make a hen and Chickens Coop. This was made by nailing the ends of two wide boards, which had been sawed on the slant, together to make a tent shaped structure. The back was boarded up and lath or slats nailed across the front far enough apart so the little chickens could go in and out but the hen had to stay inside.

They must have raised at least part of the chickens as the Yackles had Bantam chickens for many years.

Their home was almost two miles from the Germany Methodist church west of Berne. They all walked to the services. Neighbors often joined them and all would sing hymns as they wound their way toward the church.

Bible reading and prayer began their day. Later, when they had an organ, the congregation would join in singing hymns in the evening. They used. their talents through the years by singing in the choir.

The Yackle's had ten children. They were Mary, Christina, George, John, Gottlieb, Caroline, Katherine, William, Dorethea and Frieda.

(Pigeon Progress-Advance 07-07-1977)

With all the hardships they encountered in the new land, they must have had great faith and leaned heavily on Bible promises such as "As thy days so shall thy Strength be." Deut. 33:25 or "Thou will keep him in perfect peace whose mind is stayed on thee." lsa. 26:3, or maybe "Call upon me and I will answer thee and show thee great and mighty things, which thou knowest not." Jer. 33:3

As I began writing about the Yackles on February 21, 1977, word came that the l last surviving member of the family had just passed on. She was Katherine Yackle Domine, who lived to the age of 99 years and 5 months old.

The Yackle family; in the back row, George, Katherine, Mary; Christine, Caroline and John.

Mother Christine is at left in the front row; then Dorathea, Gottlieb, William, Frieda and father George.

Last summer, Mr. and Mrs. Willis Yackle visited the large, beautiful Yackle home in Germany. After I saw the picture of that home, couldn't help but compare it with the shanty. I wondered how many of the pioneer mothers left fine homes in the old country to live in shanties or log homes in the new land. Perhaps many. *(Pigeon Progress-Advance 07-14-1977)*

Taken in 1904, this photo shows August and Katie Yackle Domine on their wedding day. They were the first couple to be married in the Methodist church building. Attendants at the ceremony were Dora Yackle, Charlie Winterstine, Julia Winterstine, Will Yackle, Frieda Armbruster, Albert Henkie.

The Townships Of This Area

I recently read a short sketch about Winsor Township, and soon discovered the statement, "Winsor Township was the last in the county to be organized." This surprised me. Then after further thought I realized the statement was incorrect, I remember very distinctly when McKinley Township was organized. Consequently, I took mother's history and soon discovered the cause of the error.

She does not give the date of the organization of McKinley Township, as she did the others. Just states, "Since that early period, McKinley Township has been organized Its territory has been taken from Caseville."

Summary

The following is a summary of when the townships of this area were organized.

Caseville was first. It was organized April 2, 1860. It embraced all of the territory now occupied by Fairhaven, Grant, Lake, Brookfield, Chandler, Oliver, Winsor, and McKinley townships. Next, Fairhaven. was taken from Caseville and Sebewaing in April of 1863. Grant was organized in 1867. It was taken from Caseville by order of the Board of Supervisors.

Lake was organized a little later that same year, 1867, by a special act of legislature. It included what was later Chandler, Oliver and some of Grant.

Also in 1867, Brookfield was taken from Fairhaven. In 1879 Chandler was taken from Lake, and eight years later, 1887, Oliver. seceded from Lake. Winsor was taken from Fairhaven in 1880. McKinley was the last. It was part of Caseville until 1905. J. J. Murdoch was the first Supervisor and Joseph Smith was the clerk.

Orville Preston Chapin 1852-1940

Town Meeting Sixty Years Ago

Written by: O. P. Chapin, 1933

As the time for our annual town meeting draws near, my mind goes back to homestead days and the first town meeting that I attended in the territory of which Winsor then formed part.

My home was located at the north 1/2 of the northeast 1/4 of section 8 (Winsor). My homestead permit was dated Lansing, Michigan, July 21, 1873. In September, I raised my log house, covered it with three foot cedar shakes, stuffed the cracks with moss; filed my three months proof of settlement, moved in and in due time I was a local resident.

A long time ago! Since then sixty times has April showers developed the flowers of May! So many changes have taken place since then that little remains today as I saw it then. There was no Winsor township, territory of Winsor and that of Fairhaven was organized as one township, and carried the name of Fairhaven on the map. This made large township, extending from the northeast corner of Winsor to Bay Port, south to Kilmanagh then east to Wolfton, west to the bay shore and 1/2 mile this side of Sebewaing. There was not a horse owned in the entire township and every man who attended the town meeting on April 6, 1873 walked without a single exception. Several living in the remote parts of the township owing to distance and bad conditions of the roads, would remain with friends and go home the next day.

A small low building used as a school house in what is known as the Snell district served as a town hall. It stood on the northwest corner of the Otto Gettel farm, within ten feet of the north line. It was built of logs, crudely put together and roofed with shake shingles that were split from large cedar timber. This style of roofing served the purpose well in rainstorms, but with a drifting snow it was little better than nothing.

A homemade door hung with wooden hinges closed the only entrance which was so low that half of the voters had to stoop to enter. Five small windows, 8" x 10" glass, a floor made of rough green lumber, which after seasoning, left yawning cracks, two desks the entire length of the room and several movable benches, a small homemade desk for the teacher. A large box stove burning three foot wood, and you have a pen picture of the first school house and town hall that stood on the territory of what is now the township of Winsor.

The town board was comprised of J. W. Snell, supervisor; William Winton, clerk; Frank Thompson, Justice and Abram Harder. No caucus was held; the ballots were printed in Port Austin in blank form, with only the names of the different offices printed in. When the polls were opened the ballots were passed around and each voter filled in his ballot to suit himself. Writing with lead pencil, under difficult circumstances the larger percent of the penmanship was very poor and the spelling equally bad. Snell was frequently, spelled "Schnell", Chapin "Schapen," Harder " Arder?. One ballot I remember was written "Sed a Schmit" for Sydnye A. Smith. Some ballots were a puzzle, and being the only school teacher in the township. I frequently assisted in reading doubtful ballots.

As I look back and see how elections were conducted at that time I cannot help but feel that we were a good honest bunch of mossbacks; for regardless of the orthography, legal or otherwise, if the intentions of the voter could be determined the ballot was never thrown out.

Most of the voters remained until after the ballots were counted, for with an early return to their homestead; days and even weeks could pass without knowing the result. The following ticket was elected. For supervisor, Carl Heisterman; clerk, William Winton; treasurer, Sydney A. Smith; highway commissioner, Thomas Snell; Justice of Peace, O. P. Chapin; constables, Adam H. Harder, David Lamson, James Maharg and George Petty. *(Pigeon Progress-Advance 07-21-1977)*

At this town meeting the question of moving the county seat from Port Austin to Bad Axe was before the people. It carried in favor of Bad Axe, with a strong majority. I also remember that William H. Merrick was elected county sheriff. Forty three voters cast their ballots. Here is the list: John A. Stapleford, Thomas Abbott, J. W. Snell, John Harder, Carl Propranz, Carl Heisterman, Charles E. Grant, Peter Givels, Abram Harder, Taugott Dietzell, Sydney A. Smith, James Maharg, John Boyd, Frank Thompson, James Omich, George Taylor, Lester Demings, Carl Helmich, Micheal Shindler, August Hartman, Andrew Kuhl, Edward Jahru, Adam H. Harder, Morgan Frazer, O. P. Chapin. Alexander Grant, Fred Wasserman, Henry Muentener, John Dietzel, Henry Froebe, Herman F. Roedle, Henry Pincurnb, John Hinton, William Kappen, Thomas Hilyer, Micheal Hartman, Henry Henne, David Lamson, Henry Stockle, William Winton.

The following voters of the township who did not attend the meeting were: Alexander Stapleford, Gerome Petty, William (Bill) Moore, Edward Moore, Micheal Shoe, Dr. Schultz, John Hornbacher, Baker Johnson, John Flickinger, James Valentine, Abraham Hyzer, Peter Petty, George Huekle, George Davis, John Speidt, Daniel Dutcher, Gottlieb Glosser, Henry Mainsel, Fred Korn, Henry Moeller, Fred Jacobs, William Ribble, Charles Gillingham, Edward Tarry, Thomas Fluett, Joseph Molzer, William Hartman, Rev. Shaffer, John (Jack) Glosser, Edward Stamm, Philip Sharpstine, Peter Hyzer, Fred A. Henne, John Petty. As 1 look over the list of the non-attendants named above, they either lived on the islands, or on the sandridge near Sebewaing or east of the Pigeon River. At that time there were only two bridges by which crossings could be made, one on the north town line known as the Hoppe bridge and one on the south town line known as the Holmes bridge. In order to reach points west of the Pigeon River during the spring breakup, a difficult round-about-way had to be followed.

This in connection with treacherous ice between the islands and the mainland, together with the distance that several had to come during the early years, cut down the poll list to less than fifty voters.

Young men lacking about one year before they could legally vote were: Abraham Stapleford, Fred L. Harder, Dennis Grant, Jacob Ribble, William M. Henne, Henry Froebe, Jr., George Hyzer, Chris Hacket, William Kain, Julius Diefenbach, William Schultz and Robert Maharg.

Mckinley Township, 1904

The members of the McKinley Township board in 1904 were supervisor, John Murdoch; treasurer, B. R. Baur; clerk, Peter Webber; highway commissioner, Thomas Horn; the four justices were, Arthur White, C.F. Leipprandt, Henry Stiegman Sr., Louis Thiel; board of review, Matt Richmond and Edward Sturm; school inspectors were Charles Hoppe and Charles Stewart. The constables were Albert Steadman, Gilson Harder, Henry Domine and Martin Sturm.

The Tamarac Swamp

By the "eighties", Caseville, Bay Port and Sebewaing as well as other towns in Huron County were busy places. People had bought land and built houses until the site of Pigeon was surrounded with settlers.

Some might ask, "Why was Pigeon so long in becoming a town?" The answer is easy. "The Tamarac Swamp." People do not generally settle in swamps or start towns in them.

The story is told that 40 acres of, the swamp was at one time traded for a gun and the gun was in poor shape.

First Houses

According to Martin Sturm the only house in Pigeon, when the railroad was being built was the Chris Muentener house, which was west of the Planing Mill. The road came to it from the west. He carried water to the men who worked on the grade from the Muentener's well.

The Henry Moeller house was on their farm to the northwest. Both Muenteners and Moellers had belonged to the Ora Labora Colony which disbanded in 1857-1858. John Glosser, an old river driver, also "had a house on his 40 acres, which according to an old paper was bounded by South Main Street and Michigan Avenue.

The fourth house was built the year the railroad was completed in 1883. It was just south of the depot. It was used until 1935 when it was torn down.

Everyone agreed that the swamp was not an ideal place for a town but fate decreed differently. How it came about makes interesting reading and brings us to the fourth factor: The Railroads.

The Railroads:
Pontiac, Oxford and Northern

In 1881 the people of this section became quite excited when they heard the news that the Pontiac, Oxford and Northern was to be built from Pontiac to Caseville. It would be a great boost to the territory and it certainly was just that! First because it gave employment to many men. For instance the railroad bed had to be graded. The work was contracted for mile by mile.

In one of my Aunt Maria Gwinn's letters written to her by her brothers while she was teaching school in various places stated, "Richard (my father) is foreman of the grading between Anderson's and Newman's crossings" (Dunn and Filion Roads). "Fouls (who lived near the R.R. on Limerick Road) have the work north from their place." *(Pigeon Progress-Advance 07-28-1977)*

Many men with teams and dump scrapers, as well as others were employed. Then secondly, it gave the peoples means of transportation and the freight trains could carry supplies both ways so they did not have to rely solely on boats, which could not operate during the winter.

Again. quoting from her letters Uncle Joe wrote, "About 1000 tons of R. R. iron is coming into Caseville by boat. One boat had to be reloaded in Port Huron, as the first ship could not take the waves."

"They are hauling the iron rails into the Tamarac Swamp."

Next from one by Richard, "I rode the train as far as Bill's farm. The track is laid to the town-line" (Berne Road). The R. R. was finished in 1883 and small towns sprang up all along the line. Berne was one of them.

The trains also brought the mail. There was one coach in which a postal clerk sorted the mail as the train traveled. Mail was delivered and picked up at each depot.

When I was a child the Hayes mail was thrown off the 1:30 p.m. train, going to Caseville at the Anderson crossing. It decreased its speed so the outgoing mail bag could he thrown on and the incoming thrown off.

The first mail carrier was Richard Bailey (Clif Bailey's grandfather). When he passed on Mrs. Bailey took over the task. She had to walk over two miles each day, summer and winter, to carry the mail bag to deliver the mail to the Hayes P.O. which was established in 1876 on July the 4th. C. F. Leipprandt was the postmaster. The first Hayes P.O. was in the store which was moved to Berne in 1884. Mr. C. F. Leipprandt then built the little brick store which is just south of the John Leipprandt home. The north end was the store and the P. O. The south end was the chicken coop. Many a time I picked up our mail, after school, in that little P.O. Our box was No 15 and cost 20 cents a year. Later a larger store was built near the road and the P.O. installed there with more boxes.

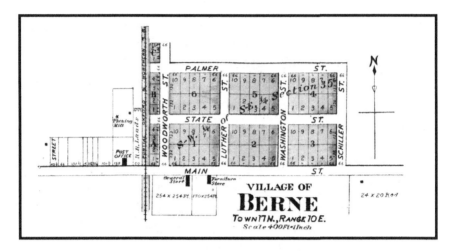

Berne Is Born

Word came in 1881 that the Pontiac, Oxford & Northern Railroad was to be built from Pontiac to Caseville. That may have been the year that Henrich Woelfel's First Addition was platted.

It consisted of six of ten lots each, plus a row of small lots bordering the railroad making a total of 72 lots. There were five avenues running north to south and three streets east to west. The avenues were: Woodworth, just east of the railroad, then Luther, Washington and Schillie. The streets were Main (Berne Road), State and Palmer.

From a map in the Huron County Plat Book of 1904, it looks as if the railroad station might have been the fourth lot north of Main Street on Woodworth Avenue. There were still four buildings along the railroad at that time, and eight buildings on the north side of Main Street. Part must have been stores originally. Besides these there were two houses on State Street and the Mennonite Church was on the corner of Washington Avenue and State Street.

The addition evidently had been bought from Fred Wolfe who owned the farm north of the addition. The homes of H. Muehler and John J. Glosser were east of the addition.

On the south side of the road was the farm of D. Diefenbach. On the corner of Main Street and the road to Pigeon was the Cider Mill, owned by W. Schultz. It was operated for several years. Just east of the Cider Mill was the large James Black store and a sawmill, originally owned by William Flinger. It was later sold to H. J. Schroeter. The H. L. Domine building was next. It could have been either a house or store, and a short distance west was the H. C. Wideman residence. Beyond it was a large building owned by F. Wolf. It may have been his home. One more house completed the homes on the north side of the street. Across the road was the Jacob Wagester farm and home. To the west was the Lutheran Church, Parsonage and school.

"The Vinegar Barrel"

Taken from "Mud Creek," written in 1967.

Each fall, Grandpa Morse and Uncle Alf would hitch up the team to the wagon, which had the box on it, drive into the orchard and begin picking apples for cider. Sweet apples and snows made the best cider. When the box was full, they drove to Berne to the mill and came home with the cider. The cider mill was a busy place, because nearly everyone had an orchard, and took their apples to the mill to be made into cider and then apple butter. They put the barrel of cider on the west porch while it changed into vinegar. In the winter it was brought inside and placed north of the couch. They supplied their family with vinegar. We would take our vinegar jug over each time it was empty to have it refilled.

"Making Apple Butter"

This was the day we looked forward to. Grandpa and Uncle Alf would have a good supply of wood, and the big black kettle clean and ready for the cider. Aunt Ida, mother, and grandma peeled the apples and got them ready to add to the cider. When the men who had been tending the fire reported the cider had boiled down enough, then the stirring began.

I don°t remember if they used the stirrer father made or not, or whether it was just used when they changed and began to make apple butter in copper boilers. Anyway, the stirrer was made of a smooth 1-inch board about 4-inches wide and 2 feet long. Father bored several rows of 3 holes, 1-inch in diameter across the board. He had a larger hole at the top of the board into which he fastened part of a fork handle. This made an excellent stirrer to keep the apple butter from catching on the bottom of the boiler.

It took careful watching and stirring near the last. Sometimes sugar was added and always cinnamon. Finally, it was pronounced ready to put into the crocks for winter keeping. Of course, the best part of the day was having a big dish of it on the table to be spread on the good homemade' bread for our supper. The vinegar jug was made of material like we made crocks out of, and I still have the jug and "the stirrer to remind me of apple butter days.

Business Places

The Pontiac, Oxford & Northern railroad was completed in 1883. In that same year, Joe Schluchter, who had been employed by the Liken Store in Old Bay Port, opened up a General Store in Berne.

It is unknown why the town was called Berne, but it is spelled the same as Berne in Switzerland and we do know the Schluchters originally came from there.

In 1884, W. and E. G. Leipprandt moved their General Store from the farm of C. Leipprandt in Hayes to Berne. While in Hayes, the store sold everything from watches to wagons. Both Schluchter and Leipprandt purchased grain. Simon Hoffman's may have also been a General Store, but he at least carried hardware, because when the Mud Creek brick school was built in 1884, they bought zinc nails and bolts from him.

Soon other places of business opened in Berne, which had a hotel run by Pat Quinn. Fred Daufner had a blacksmith and wagon shop. My father bought his first single buggy from him. It was a high, side spring buggy with no top. I well remember that buggy. Father weighed more than mother, so father's side was always lower than mothers.

Finally one day while going out to Uncle Sam's in Chandler, the side spring on father's side broke. Luckily we were opposite Anderson's woods on Limerick Road and their rail fence. So father found a rail, which he pushed under his side of the buggy, and on we went with the rail protruding out behind.

The town had three blacksmiths, because oxen and horses had to have shoes in order to work in the woods during the winter. Louis Rather was one blacksmith and Robert Brown another. He was Anna Beach's grandfather. After Pigeon began to grow he moved his shop to a farm on the southeast corner of Gagetown and Filion Roads. I was in that Blacksmith shop as a small child, when I visited my cousin, Anna. How well I remember having to go with Anna and Bert up to Fred Steinman's with a message from their father. It was dusk when we started over the old narrow corduroy road, that traveled through swamps. The water, with the tall cat-tails and trees. was almost as high as the logs in the road. We were afraid, so we ran both ways in order to get home before dark.

Berne also had a cabinet maker, his name was Charles Solter. There was also a cobbler, Mr. Soldon. Cobblers were busy people in those days. One's shoes had to be worn as long as possible. So when a hole developed in the side of the shoe or in the sole, it was taken to the cobbler. He put on a patch or new soles as needed. He also straightened the heels and the shoes would last a long time, but they were very stiff at first.

Vena Hoppe had a Millinery shop, and was also a dressmaker. Berne also had a Post Office. Joe Schluchter was the first post master. When he moved his store to Pigeon 1895, the Post Office was discontinued. I can faintly remember hearing of the dissatisfaction of the Berne residents at the losing of their Post Office. It was later restored. James Black was the post master and the Post Office was in his store.

It was quite a thriving town! I have letters sent to my Aunt Marie Gwinn, when she taught the Turner School. Her address was Berne,

Michigan. Written by Florence Gwinn Schluchter

James Black's store was on the South side of Main Street. The Post Office was there at least until 1904. G. V. Black, as stated, came at a later date. His store was the North side of Main Street.

The Mail

The Post Office in Berne was established on May 29, 1882, and operated for fourteen years until it was discontinued on October 2, 1896. The following May, however, the post office was re-activated and remained. in service to the area until April 8, 1904. After that time, mail for Berne came to Pigeon, Rural Free Delivery came into being and Berne was served by Rural Route NO. 1.

The first mailman was John Foster. He had a single buggy with a top and drove two black horses. He used one of them one day and the other the next. During the winter he used a cutter.

After a few years. Henry Horn became the mailman. He was followed by Edward j. Anklam. who served for 41 years. His son Calvin succeeded him and is the present mailman. Calvin has served for 23 years.

Ed, as he was called, was a very obliging person, and always had a cheery greeting for everyone. Calvin has inherited some of his father's characteristics.

The early years had their problems. Roads were often very muddy and during the winter when the snow came the roads were not plowed out as they are today.

Often those first mailboxes had little shelves where pennies could be placed if one did not have a stamp or post card. Letters required a two-cent stamp and post cards, one cent.

Often in the winter time; snow would blow into the mailboxes and cover the pennies. Mr. George Newman Sr. wrote a poem about the era entitled "Picking Pennies Out of The Snow."

It was 1916 when Eddie Anklam (above) replaced Henry Horn as the rural mail carrier for Pigeon route 1, which covered a distance of

30 miles. In the horse and buggy days, he changed tires twice on the route ... the first time at John Maxwell's and later at Gust Bergman's. Only six autos were on the route when Ed started ... he himself used an auto when road conditions permitted. There were only three miles of improved roads at the time. and mud and snow often made them impassable for cars. Ed had the above snow-mobile rigged up to get him through his appointed rounds.

Eddie delivered everything from mail to hard coal and chickens. He even brought 12 yards of material to Clara Scheurer for pinafores one day when her doctor husband was in surgery and couldn't get home as promised. Ed figured at one time, that he wore out 17 automobiles and traveled more than 20 times the distance around the world in his 40 years of service.

St. John's Evangelical Lutheran Church

St. John's Evangelical Lutheran Congregation was founded on September 8, 1878 by Pastor C. Boehner as a traveling missionary. Services were at first held in a log house on the banks of the Pigeon River, where Jacob Swartzendruber now lives (1947). The congregation was first served b Rev. C. F. Boehner and by the pastors from

Sebewaing, Rev. H. Gangnuss and the Rev. G. Turk. In 1882, Pastor V. F. Menke, became the regular pastor. In 1885, a parsonage was built as well as the old church. This was built by Mr. M. Heinemann for $1,150. The new church was build in 1917.

In 1888, Pastor Menke accepted a different call and the Rev. R. Praetorius became pastor of the congregation. He was followed in 1891 by Rev. W. Linsenmann of Waterloo, Michigan. In 1895, Pastor G. F. Wacker became pastor of the congregation and in 1896 the old school was built. The new school was built in 1935. Pastor G. F. Wacker died in 1936. The present pastor A. W. Hueschen came in 1936.

During the past eleven years intensive and extensive improvements have been made in every department of the congregations work. Over 400 souls, 283 communicant members, 81 voting members, 67 children in Sunday school. And an active Ladies Aid Society. (Written by Rev. A. W. Hueschen, 1947).

Salem Evangelical Church

The beginning of the Salem Evangelical church dates back to the year 1885, when Rev. D. W. Schafer established a preaching place in the home of Mr. Louis Thiel (on the northeast corner of Berne and Sturm Roads). A Sunday School was organized in 1886. Rev. G. J. Kirn served the field as junior preacher, associated with Rev. Peter Allen. The Sunday School grew and larger quarters were found in the Turner School House (on the northeast corner of Berne and Gagetown Roads). Rev. W. F. Vogel came as the next pastor and under his labors a class of twenty charter members was organized.

At this time the field was made a part of the Elkton Circuit. The first church building was erected in Berne in 1891. W. A. Bulgrin, B. F. Wade and W. Berge served as pastors in the order indicated. During Brother Berge's pastorate the church building was moved to Pigeon. (Written by Rev. L. A. Ruegsegger).

German M. E. Church

The Ebenezer Mission was organized in 1871. The Mission included all the territory from Caseville to Kilmanagh, and was the ministered by Circuit Riders and two local preachers, C. F. Leipprandt. The Berne District of the Ebenezer Mission met one mile west and one-fourth mile north of Pigeon in the home of a member. Blocks of wood and long planks were set up so everyone would have a place to sit. There were no musical instruments to sing by, so when the leader was ready to begin a hymn, he would raise his hand for quiet. The congregation could then hear the hum of thousands of mosquitoes flying in the room, which designated the key of C. In 1872, the Pigeon River Church was built one mile west of Pigeon on the east side of the River. The Central German Conference in 1872, assigned the area's first regularly appointed pastors of the River Church.

It took the congregation only four years to outgrow the Pigeon River Building. They decided to purchase two and a half acres of land on the northwest corner of North Caseville and Berne Roads. The land was donated by Frances Crawford at a cost of $1.09 for the deed, which stated that if the property was not used for a church it would revert back to him.

The first bell in the area rang from the steeple of that church. The interior of the church was arranged according to old German custom, with a dividing partition through the center of each pew. The women and children sat on one side of the partition and the men on the other. In 1892, the Epworth League was organized. It was a fellowship for old and young.

In 1872, the church had eleven preparatory members, 23 fall members, six Sunday School teachers, Sunday School enrollment of thirty. Benevolence $3.55. By 1902, they had two preparatory members, 129 full members, 28 Sunday School, teachers and Sunday School enrollment of 140. Benevolence $185.00.

The pastors who served the G. M. church were: George Henry

Maentz 1872-1874 Joseph Kern 1874-1876 Louis Christian 1876-1878 William F. Henke 1878-1881 Andrew Kruemling 1881-1883 Daniel Volz 1883-1884 Oscar Rogatsky 1884-1887 Herman Rogatsky 1887-1888 Andrew Mayer 1888-1892 Christian Spaeth 1892-1897 Henry Bank 1897-1898.

The church moved to Pigeon in 1898. *Information from Centennial Program.*

This incident happened when mother was teaching in the German Settlement, (Winsor School). She had been home over the weekend as usual and Sunday afternoon Uncle Rob was taking her back to her boarding place. Uncle Rob loved good driving horses. That year he had a very nice team, which he hitched to the sleigh. The sleigh was just large enough for two seats. He asked some girl to ride with him in the front seat and Tom Smith to ride with mother in the back seat.

The German M. E. church, was on the Berne corner. Church Service was just over and the people outside, as they drove past. Uncle Rob decided it was a good time to show off his team, so he tiped the horses with the whip. They dashed forward with such speed that it caused the sleigh to give a jerk. Over went the back seat. Tom, mother and the robe were deposited in the snow. How the people laughed! Uncle Rob unaware that he had lost his passengers sped on up the road. Tom tried to call but his voice was drowned by the laughter. Nothing left to do but pick up the seat and robe and start walking after the sleigh, much to the amusement of the crowd. Finally, Uncle Rob discovered their plight and returned to pick them up.

The Cemetery

Nearly 50 years had passed since the congregation moved from Berne to Pigeon. With the abandonment of the Berne church, the cemetery was also neglected. By now only the older members were conscientious of the responsibility the church had for the burial grounds of its ancestors. The cemetery had became a weed-choked tangle of brush and fallen trees. In 1961, the church decided to do something about it. After months of studying old church records, and contacting next of kin, work began. The brush was burned off; revealing toppled tombstones. As the project progressed financial help and volunteer labor began to come in. Tree stumps up to four feet in diameter were blasted out. Tombstones were hauled away. Bulldozers swept up remaining debris and leveled the ground.

Finally, in the fall of 1962, the plot 'was seeded to grass. The largest tombstone from the cemetery was refinished and the names of the sixty-two pioneers, who rested in the cemetery were cut into it.

Mennonite Church

When Huron County was still a wooded country, the first Mennonites to settle this section were Mr. and Mrs. William Bechtel. In December of 1888 Mr. and Mrs. Peter Ropp came from Canada and settled on a farm on Campbell Road (Bay Port address). Soon there were other families who followed.

These early families had to use their wagons and sometimes ox teams as they traveled the River Road or trails through the woods. Even though their transportation was not like ours of today they wanted a church service. They held their first meeting in the William Bechtel home January 13, 1890. The service was conducted by Rev. Dan Lehman from Fairgrove, Michigan.

For the next few years a minister from Canada came occasionally and preached for them.

It was not until 1894 that a church was organized, at the home of Mr. and Mrs. John Oesch, by Rev. David Wissmer of Berlin, Canada (now known as Kitchener).

At the same time a Sunday school was organized. The first S. S. Supts. were Elias Weidman and Joel Reist. The Charter members of the church were: Mr. and Mrs. William Bechtel, Mr. and Mrs. Peter Ropp, Mr. and Mrs. Elias Weidman, Mr. and Mrs. Moses Weidman, Mr. and Mrs. Joseph Ropp, Mr. and Mrs. Christian Bechler, Mr. and Mrs. Joel W. Heist, Mr. and Mrs. John Oesch, Mr. and Mrs. Isreal

Dettiweiler, Mr. and Mrs. John Roth and others.

As they continued to meet in the various homes, they realized their need of a church building and as Berne was the town at that time a church was built in Berne in 1897, on the corner of State Street and Washington Avenue.

It was a small frame church. The front of the church faced the east. The pulpit was in the center with a door on each side and a small rooms for coats. The ladies entered through the north door, the men through the south. There was also a door on the west end. There were short pews on each side against the wall and a center section of longer home-made pews, with an aisle on each side. The men and boys occupied the pews on the south side and the ladies and girls those on the north.

When the church was completed a Dedication service was held. It was conducted by Samuel Bowman in June, 1897. In July of the same year Peter Ropp was ordained as minister. On the same date Menno Weidman was ordained as a deacon. Those services were conducted by Bishop Amos Cressman and Samuel Bowman from New Hamburg, Ontario.

One Sunday as Peter Ropp was preaching, Daniel Schultz, who was the minister of the Mennonite church in Elkton, stepped through the door. Mr. Ropp stopped preaching and said, "Mr. Schultz come and preach to them." He came up and asked, "What is your Text?" When told he immediately started to preach and gave a good sermon on that Text. (Something few could do).

In the meantime, more people moved into the community with their families. Some of these were: Andrew Schaaf, Moses Heckendorn, Ben Bowman, John Kipfer, Daniel Steckly, J. W. Roth, Chris Ropp, John Ulrich, Abram Snyder.

At their first Revival Meetings were held 1898 by David Garber at which time twelve converts were received into the church.

About 1904 a small addition was added to the church to make room for the growing congregation.

For several years Revival Services were held during the summer in a tent, which was put up near the church. In 1934 the church moved to Pigeon.

The church in Berne was still owned by the church and used by the Youth Fellowship and for other activities in the early 1970's.

The cemetery in McKinley township was donated by Henry E. Weidman from his 40 acre farm.

Thanks to Mrs. William Bechler for doing the research on the history of the Mennonite church.

The S. T.& H. Railroad

When the Saginaw, Tuscola and Huron Railroad was built as far as Sebewaing in 1883, and then on to "The Quarry" in 1884 folks decided it surely would not go thru the Tamarac Swamp but would cross the P.O. and Northern at Berne. Consequently Berne began to boom! To the dismay of many especially the Berne merchants the S. T. & H. crossed the P.O. & N. 1 mile south of Berne, right thru the Tamarac swamp. The crossing was called Berne Junction.

The S. T. & H. R. R. was sold to the Pere Marquette in 1890, when W. H. Wallace was the superintendent.

For several years they ran special excursion trains to the then flourishing Bay Port Resort. The many coaches would be jammed with passengers.

One fourth of July, I rode one of those trains coming home from Bay Port. The train traveled at a snails pace as far as the quarry to give the conductor time to pick up the tickets.

Later the Pere Marquette was sold to the Chesapeake and Ohio.

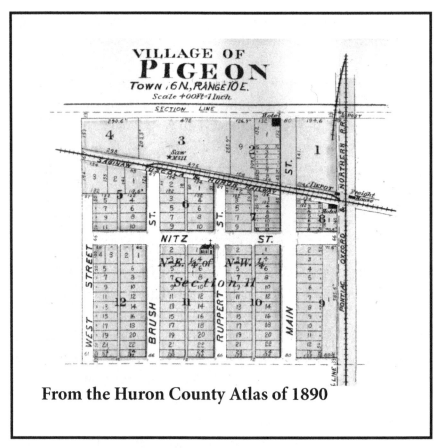

From the Huron County Atlas of 1890

Berne Junction

Charles Applegate was the first station agent at Berne Junction. He evidently had a better vision, than most, as to what the place might become, because he persuaded John Nitz, whose farm was south of Berne Junction to help plat the Nitz and Applegate Plat. It is South and West of Michigan Ave. and Main St.

The First Store

Mr. Applegate also built the first store in 1887. It was quite a large two story building on the N. E. corner of S. Main and Nitz St. The library occupies that site at present. He carried a small stock of merchandise

Leipprandt Bros. of Berne purchased the Applegate building the
next year (1888) and operated it as a branch store. Leipprandt's
store is far right with the banner sign above the door.

Post Office Established

It was also in 1890 that the Pigeon Post Office was established with
Albert Kleinschmidt as Postmaster. He held that position, with the
exception of four years, (when his brother Herman was postmaster)
until George Anklam was a pointed during President Wilson's first
administration. The Post Office was on the north side of Michigan
Avenue, the first building west of N. Main St. It was later Witwer's
Harness Shop and still later Mose Haist's Tailor Shop. (The P. O. at
one time was moved into a building on the spot of Niebel's Grocery
of 1977).

The Maccabees built the K. O. T. M. Hall next to the P. O. on West
Michigan Ave. It was used for their meetings, shows and town meetings. After a few years it was Jack Diebel's Hardware Store.

The building to the east of the P. O. was Mr. Wooley's Millinery
and on the corner was Silas Bedford's residence on the site of the Bank
of today. *(Pigeon Progress-Advance 08-14-1977)*

Jim Spence's Seed Store and S. W. Witwer, harness maker are located center - Left. The Bedford home is located right, where the bank is located now.

Three more additions in 1888 to the struggling little town were The Union Station, John Diebel's Planing Mill east of the P. O. & N. track in the Diebel addition and the John McNiel Store, which was built next to the Leipprandt Store. He sold to G. C. Heineman in 1893. Mr. Heineman carried on a furniture and undertaking business for six years. (The bedroom furniture in my room was purchased from Mr. Heineman by my grandfather, Robert Morse. G.C. Heineman's name is on the back of the dresser) *(Pigeon Progress-Advance 08-25-1977)*

Other Buildings 1888

That same year Joe Schluchter of Berne opened a store in a building on the west side of S. Main, and also ran it as a branch store. It was about where the Schumacher Market is today.

Still another business place of that era was William Goff's Harness Shop. It was on the S. W. corner of S. Main and Nitz Streets. Little by

The Arlington was the first hotel. It was built by Herman Kleinschmidt on the southwest corner of Michigan Avenue and Main Street in 1888. Later, it was sold to George Winter and then to Robert McElmurray and Lee Elenbaum.

Diebel's mill, on the site now occupied by Pigeon Co-Op offices.

Lumber from Diebel's mill being delivered with horse and wagon.

little the town was growing.

More growth took place in 1890. Liken and Bach of Sebewaing bought John Diebel's Saw Mill and converted it into a Stave and Heading Plant. That same year John Diebel built the planing mill. Today the Co-op Office building occupies that space.

Growth In 1892

Both the Methodist Episcopal and Presbyterian churches were erected in 1892, on the east side of Main St. A flax factory was also constructed on the west side of Berne St. and north of Charles St. Ernest Paul was the manager. At one time they employed 42 men. Later Jim Bright was the manager. That same year a Creamery was built but it burned down the next year.

In1894 Louis Staubus came from Dashwood Ontario, Canada and started a Shoe Repairing and Shoe Store, which he operated for many years.

Wallace and Orr elevator beside the then Pere Marquette R. R.
(Above Left). They carried on the business for many years.
It was demolished to make space for the Free Parking Lot of today.

1895 The Boom Year

In the streets of Pigeon, a farmer and his wagon were photographed in the late 1890s or early 1900s.

Henry Moeller Sr. plotted the N. W. section of town in 1895 as The Moeller addition. The Crawford Estate platted the N. E. Section the same year as The Crawford Addition.

Both Leipprandt's and Joe Schluchter closed their Berne Stores that year.

The K. O. T. M.(Macabee) Hall mentioned before was also built in 1895.

During the winter of 1895; 17 houses were moved from Berne to Pigeon on the snow. Each house had to have a board sidewalk from the house to the street because of the mud, even though the swamp had been drained.

When the frost went out in the spring the streets had mud half way to the hub of the wagon wheels.

Another building erected that year was one built by Wallace and Orr, who put in a stock of general merchandise. The next year they sold it to Joe Schluchter.

Wallace and Orr also built an elevator beside the then Pere Marquette R. R. They carried on the business for many years. It was demolished to make space for the Free Parking Lot of today.

The William Leipprandt white brick home on Michigan Ave. was also built that same year. The family moved in just before Christmas.

As a climax to all the other progress the town had made, F. W. Hubbard opened. "The Farmer's Bank" on the site of the present Oesch Shoe Store. F .W. Merrick was the cashier. Later it became the Pigeon State Bank.

In 1901 Ernest Clabuesch was engaged as janitor clerk and chore boy. By 1915 he became cashier, then later Vice President and finally President.

He retired December 23, 1974 after 73 years in the banking busi-

Auto club members were getting ready to go to Bay City. The Farmers' Bank is located on the far right. The home on the left has been moved to Berne Street and the Shell Station is now located on that corner.

ness. *(Pigeon Progress-Advance 09-01-1977)*

Up until 1895, all buildings were frame but when William Heasty and John A. McLean built the Heasty Hotel they used white brick. The three story addition was added in 1911.

Mr. Heasty ran the north half of the building as a hotel and John A. McLean used the south half as a store. (John A. was Walter McLean's father).

Meals at that time consisted of meat, bread, potatoes, two side dishes and a piece of pie. The cost was 25 cents. A bed for the night cost $1.00.

Heasty Hotel with employees standing outside.

The hotel is the oldest building in Pigeon today.

Mailed in 1912, this postcard shows the "hot rods" of the day displaying typical disregard for the flow of traffic in front of the Heasty House on South Main Street in Pigeon.

A town growing as fast as Pigeon needed a Grist Mill so Leipprandt Bros. built one in 1895 beside the P.O. & N. R.R. north of Michigan Ave. Later they added the elevator.

After carrying on the business for many years they sold to the Pigeon Coop.

Mr. Will Leipprandt took his daughter, Ruth, along when they drove to Grindstone City to purchase the stone for the Grist Mill.

In the early days, wheat was "stone ground" and was rough in texture. In order to preserve the usefulness of the grindstones, which were worn smooth with making flour, grooves were cut into the stone to make them rough again. This early grist mill had the capacity of 50 barrels of flour a day.

Lillian Sturm Leipprandt remembers seeing, her father Martin Sturm load the wagon with wheat and empty flour barrel to go to the mill. He would return with the barrel of flour and a bag of bran.

1898

Liken and Bach, who owned the Stave and Heading Plant sold it to Joe Schluchter, who in turn disposed of the property to W. L. Harlacher and Albert Hartley. They used the main building as a Planing Mill. A short time later they added a lumber yard.

A little later Mr. Harlacher became the sole owner. Today it is the "Pigeon Lumber & Supply Co."

The elevator and flour mill are pictured on a postcard, mailed in 1909. This would become the Co-Op elevator in 1915. The low building in the center was the power plant for the mill.

This article was taken from the Pigeon Progress,
dated October 8, 1898.

The Grist Mill

A Great Industry Added to Our Town
One That Our People Should Feel Proud of

Last Tuesday morning the new grist mill started to grind its first wheat, and what is remarkable is that the wheels started at 7 o' clock and continued to run until 6 without a stop. Very seldom a mill runs ten hours without any trouble the first day. That goes to show what first class work and good machinery does.

The mill is now running every day grinding out as good flour as can be produced, and long may she do her faithful work.

The machinery has a capacity of eighty barrels per day, and is an institution that Pigeon can feel proud of. The building throughout is nicely arranged, and when the few finishing touches are put on, which is being as rapidly done as possible, no finer grist mill can be found in the state.

Mr. Leitz, a miller of long experience, is employed to do what his trade calls for, and Fred Reithel will act as engineer.

The Pigeon Milling Co., composed of three of our enterprising business men, J.W. Leipprandt, E.C. Leipprandt and Fred Reithel, have erected this mill at an expense of about $10,000. They have spared no pains in order to make a beautiful building and put in up-to-date machinery. Now as the industry will be a great trade builder for our town, every citizen should see that he is interested in its welfare. There is one way that all can show their appreciation of the efforts of the proprietors and that is by using none other than, which will soon be, the celebrated White Rose Flour.

Memories Of Our Rides To Pigeon
1897 To 1904

When I was a child a trip to town was an experience we enjoyed. Because of the slow pace, of the horse and buggy days, one had plenty of time to notice the interesting things along the way.

In 1897 our house consisted of just the center section and a small kitchen on the north. We would leave with our butter and eggs to barter for our needs and would drive out our lane, then open the gate so we could drive out on the road (all farms were fenced).

The Schluchter home was in the orchard S.E. of the barn. By 1904 the house was moved to the present site' and an addition built on the north. Our home also boasted of a wing on the south by that time.

As we made our way down the road, we passed the Leipprandt woods which bordered the Schluchter farm and the road.

William Gwinn's barn and small two story frame house were next, beside the woods along the river flats. It was always interesting crossing the bridge. There might be turtles on the log which extended into the water, or a fish might jump on the north side. Also in the fall we might occasionally see a muskrat or two and on rare occasions a mink.

I'm not sure if the new iron bridge had replaced the old wooden bridge, which was built on piles driven into the ground, or not but I do know I was afraid to drive in the north side road ditch and then thru the water to the west side of the river while the new bridge was being built.

Today the children call the iron bridge 'The Thunder Bridge'.

Half way to the corner was the big oak tree on the north side of the road. This was where the gypsies camped when they passed thru the country in the summertime. It was an ideal spot as there was no ditch on that side of the road and their horses could feed on the grass. C. F. Leipprandt had planted lombardi popular trees from about even with the oak tree around the road to the Hayes School house. These had grown to be big trees at that time.

As we turned south on Sturm Road, George Anderson's barbed wire fence around his farm was made of the first kind of barbed wire ever made. It was a flat wire about 1/3 inch wide with barbs a short distance apart on each side and the wire was twisted.

Leipprandt's home and buildings were next. One barn was built facing the road. When threshing, the engine had to sit partly on the road and horses were afraid of the engine. William Gwinn's barn was the same.

The Leipprandt drive was about where it is today. On the north side was a walk lined with shrubs and flowers. Near the house one walked thru a grape arbor. French lilacs surrounded the house. The Post Office and store were in the small brick building south of the house and an orchard was South of the drive.

Anderson's woods were across the road and held one°s attention perchance one might see a rabbit or a couple of squirrels.

The Hayes brick school house on the east was next, with its fenced acre playground and its "tall" flagpole. In the summer Gregory's brindle cow pastured in the school yard.

A short distance south was the Gregory home. The big oak trees and the other trees in front of the house were a good size at that time.

Bailey 's little red house was a short distance beyond. They had many lilacs in front of their home. These were beautiful in the spring.

The next thing of interest, especially in the spring and fall, was the Handy orchard on the east.

After the first Hayes Methodist Episcopal Church was erected in 1898, and the sheds built, we always admired our new church as we drove past.

Rounding the bend of the river we feasted our eyes on the white and yellow water lilacs, when in bloom. *(Pigeon Progress-Advance 09-15-1977)*

Next the large frame house Detrick Schubach had built with white lilacs and other shrubs on the north edge of the yard plus the flower garden in front of the house held our interest. Apple trees were all around the house. They too were beautiful spring and fall.

George Schubach had married Mary Langley. They with their children lived in a log house south of the Loren Gettel present home. The brick home' was built in 1898. My mother went with Mrs. Schubach to Detroit where they selected the furniture for the new home. W. A. Schreiber had given them a letter of introduction to the Wholesale House. I still have the nice set of hand painted bread and butter plates Mrs. Schubach gave mother for her assistance. Fred Schubach's land joined George's. Fred 's first house was a smaller oblong two story building. He had married Annie Bill. A little later they added to and bricked the house of today.

Arthur White's home was south of D. Schubach's on the Crown Road and William Horn Sr.'s home was also on the Crown Road south side.

The Steadman farms were on both sides of the Sturm Road. The one on the West was rented to J. Fox for five years. There was a large vineyard on that farm. When we Junior girls were in Mrs. Foxes Sunday School Class she held a party for us. We were allowed to pick bunches of those delicious grapes to eat. They sold the grapes in many places. County Fair's were a good market. Also the Elkton and Sebewaing Fairs.

By 1904 Henry Sturm and wife (Amelia Schubach) had bought the Steadman farm on the east side of the road. He built the brick home on that property.

Win S. Gregory, who married Jennie Stewart, lived in the next home. Their children were Lyman and Fern. The house has been extended with an addition on the north side.

Across from Gregory's was the Shaffer farm and home. I always feasted my eyes on their beautiful bleeding heart in their yard, (when it was in bloom). I have never seen a more beautiful bleeding heart.

Next were the Thiel and Bill homes, but they were on Campbell Road so the next place of interest was the Sturm home on the east side of the road. Mr. and Mrs. August Sturm lived in their log home and their son Edward had built a frame cottage type of house for his bride, Lena Damm. I had heard the gun rumor so I was always watching to see if I could see Mr. Sturm. I did a few times but of course he did not have his gun.

George Yackle, whose wife was the former Louise Schubach, had built a new brick home on the west side of the road. The now Wayne Sturm home.

The Martin Sturm home was just to the south. It was another of the new brick homes of that era. Mrs. Sturm was the former Christina Yackle. The family had planted trees and shrubs around the new house.

Beyond M. Sturms was the Elias Weidman home. The beautiful peonies in their yard always caught my eye.

In the next mile on the east side was the George Niebel brick home. He too had married a Schubach girl, Lena. Their daughter Dena lived with Joe Schubachs one year so she and I, used to walk to the Hayes School together.

Beyond Niebels was the Domine white brick home and next to the Domine home the John George Yackle's lived in an oblong two story house with a lovely garden. In those days they had little square beds of flowers with paths between the beds where one could walk. After the house was demolished, the lilacs and tiger lilies still grew along the ditch bank for many years.

In 1905 the Yackle's moved to their now Jim Mallory home in Pigeon and their son John lived in they old home for a while.

(Pigeon Progress-Advance 09-22-1977)

Attorneys-At-Law

Paul Woodworth for a short time was one of the attorneys at law, after returning from Alaska looking for gold. Alfred H. Sauer was also one, he later went to Bad Axe.

Dentist

The dentist for Pigeon and the area was Dr. Perry Fritz. He served the community for many, many years.

Father Bernard Kirchman, Doctor Perry L. Fritz, Ernst Clabuesch.
Pigeon Progress - Advance - January 12, 1962

Doctors

The first doctor was Dr. Frenzel, who practiced for many years. He built his office and house which belongs to George Dunn. Dr. Kaulmeyer was another doctor, who was here by 1901, at least as he was the pitcher of the baseball team at that time. A little later Doctor Wiley, Dr. Morrison and Dr. Dawson practiced medicine in Pigeon for some years.

Other Places Of Business

Other business in the Pigeon area included, Witwers Harness, Mrs. A Wooley's Millinery, Sururus, Ed Bundso Hardware, Hagget, Fisher, Gotthardt were blacksmiths. W. W. Loosemore's Meat Market (Mr. Loosemore used to come around to the farmers to buy cattle and hogs. He drove a spotted horse hitched to a buckboard.) D. C. McDonald coal, which was later sold to Mr. Mitehener., Fred M. Warner Cheese Factory, Frank Kinch Butter Factory and Fred Clabuesch Harness Shop.

The Gould Buggy Factory

Another thing of which Pigeon boasted in the early days was Gould's Buggy Factory. It was a large brick building east of the Pontiac, Oxford and Northern railroad near the new telephone building of today. Harry Gould did quite a business for awhile. We bought our surrey from him. Father made the deal, and that afternoon he and mother left with the team. One horse was hitched to the single buggy and our Jersey cow tied to the back of the buggy. The cow was part of the pay for the surrey. It was almost dark when we spied the folks coming home. We really ran to meet them, so we could have a ride in the new surrey the rest of the way home. Such a thrill. We felt that it was a wonderful surrey, with its two oil lamps, side curtains and the steps with mud splashers over the wheels, which made it so easy to get in, the back seat. Mr. Gould also platted

Above: Black's General Store in early 1900s

The Gould Addition

After awhile the Buggy Factory was closed because of lack of business and the big building was left vacant for some time. Then G. V. Black of Berne, moved his stock into the factory. He really did a big business! Black's Bargains were known far and wide. Later, however, in February, 1925, a fire destroyed the building and its contents.

After a few years James Spence bought the Pigeon Telephone Company from Campbell.

The business remained in the Spence family until quite recently.

Black's store was consumed in flames during the fire that destroyed it in 1925. Photographs were published in the Pigeon Progress showing the former Gould Buggy Factory consumed in flames. *(Pigeon Progress-Advance 10-06-1977)*

The Commons

For many years the land between the railroads and Michigan Avenue and Main Street was the "Commons". Silas Bedford lived in a house which occupied the site of the Thumb National Bank and Trust Company. They kept a cow in a stable a short distance in back of the house. During the summer they staked their cow on the "Commons" so she could feed on the grass. (No need for a lawnmower). The "Commons" was the spot where the "Big Wixon Shows" would put up a tent for a week each summer. Later, it was The Kelly Shows that came each year.

Everyone was excited when the shows came to town! They drew quite large crowds.

Exciting shows came to Pigeon by way of the train. Pictured above two carnivals which came into town. In the early years, these events were held in the Commons.

Farm Machinery Day

A few years following 1900, a Farm Machinery Delivery Day was quite an event in the new town. The "Dealers" H. H. Gould and Campbell and Paul, each tried to outdo the other. H. H. Gould was the McCormick dealer and Campbell and Paul the Champion dealers. Each tried to have the biggest parade led by a band. Farmers who purchased equipment were provided free meals and drinks.

Above image of Farm Implement Day was taken at the turn of the century. The Commons are at the left, and Arlington Hotel is at the far right. In the left background is Wallace Orr's Pigeon Elevator.

Freeland: The Photographer

Just when Mr. Freeland came to Pigeon, I am not sure but I do know that when the Richard Gwinn's Sr. observed their A Golden Wedding Anniversary on July 7., 1898, he took the family pictures. Soon after that the family pictures became very popular.

He had his studio on the southwest corner of South Main and Nitz Streets, where the Shell Gas Station is today. South Main Street, circa 1910, shows the shop of Freeland the photographer in the right foreground. It has been the good fortune of future generations to have

Image of South Main showing church and Freeland Studio at right.

had a photographer in the village to record on film it's earliest years and pioneer families.

(Pigeon Progress-Advance 10-13-2017)

Right: Posing for the photographer in their best coats and hats are (front row) Frieda Yackle and Flora Richmond; (second row) Mary Richmond and Miss Brodie,; (back row) Kate McDonald, Florence Come and Mae White (Green)

Mae White was learning the Millinery trade in Jessie Shaw's Millinery Shop at that time. She later had a Millinery Shop in Caseville.

In 1900, the year Hirshberg's opened their Big Store, the rivalry for the millinery business was brisk. Notter's and Hirshberg's both used large front page advertisements in the Pigeon Progress to acquaint the villagers with their stylish products. A note in a paper of that year expressed concern that birds would soon be extinct because women were using their feathers so extensively to decorate their hats.

The Jessie Notter Millinery Shop

How I loved to go to the Millinery Shop! We generally went in the spring, because in those days hats weren't worn very frequently' during the winter at least that was the custom out in the country. Women wore fasinators. They were square in shape and knit of a fine yarn in a rather open design. They were folded diagonally and tied around the head.

Children wore hoods. When I was a very small child the Milliners carried a few bonnets for the elderly ladies.

It was in the spring that the hens would lay enough eggs to fill the 12 dozen crate plus a few extra dozen. These could be bartered for a new hat. It was a long time to wait until the hens laid the eggs, but

Hirshberg's Big Store

finally they did and we went to the Shop, with its boxes and boxes of straw hats. A display case held all kinds of flowers and ribbons.

There were always a few hats that were already trimmed but they were generally too high a price for the number of eggs we had, so we would begin to try on the various shapes and sizes in the boxes until we found one to our liking. Next the very important decision as to how to have it trimmed. It was so hard to decide with so many beautiful flowers and also pick something in our price range. Sometimes it just had to be a ribbon around the crown of the hat, with the two ends extending over the brim at the back.

Then, the milliner had to trim the hat as you waited but you finally came home with a new hat. *(Pigeon Progress-Advance 10-20-1977)*

When Hirshberg's first came to Pigeon, they had a store in what was later the 'Staubus Shoe Store'. Because they had a good business, they decided to build the Big Store on Michigan Avenue. It was a two story, red brick building.

At that time, Silas Bedford lived on the 'bank corner' of today. Walter Bedford often related the following, "The night before the opening of the new store, Mr. Hirshberg and his four sons carried all the stock from the old store to the new one. I could hear them as they walked back and forth on the board sidewalks all night long. By morning they had the entire stock moved."

It was a really modern store: part of the west side of downstairs had no ceiling; That gave room for a system of wires which ran up to the cashier and bookkeeper in her office on the second floor.

Little boxes were attached to these wires which were just above the counters. After a sale the clerk put the slip and money into the boxes. By pulling a lever the box ran up to the office, where change was made if necessary. Slips and change were put back into the box and sent back to the clerk. At one time Mabel Dunn sat in that office as cashier. She could overlook both floors.

The stairway was about in the center of the store. The grocery department was in the northeast corner of the building. Sam Stead-

Silas Bedford house on center right.

man had charge of that department for awhile. Shoes occupied the southeast section.

As one entered the store the big show case with all its beautifu

Hirshberg's Interior View of Original Store

Hirshberg's Interior View of New Store

articles always was the point of interest. Dry goods were on the west side. Upstairs, the clothing and millinery departments were. I don't remember where the other departments were located.

At one time Ann Gwinn was the milliner and Bertha Schultz and Mary Schluchter were clerks as well as the four Hirshberg sons.

The Hirshberg slogan was "Everything for the Family". How do I remember the slogan? The store gave small Christmas gifts each year and one year it was a broom holder. I still have it. The slogan is on the holder.

The Silas Bedford house, later bought by Jack Diebel and moved one lot to the north and finally demolished when the bank expanded.

(Pigeon Progress-Advance 10-27-1977)

Seldom seen are these views of the interior of Hirshberg's Big Store Pictured are the bolts of cloth in the dry goods department and the cases of ribbon and trim nearby.

Many homes around Pigeon may still have many souvenirs of Hirshberg's Big Store. The directory of Pigeon in the Huron County Atlas, 1904, is the following listing: *A. Hirshherg and Son, dealer in general merchandise, a full line of shoes, cloaks, carpets, groceries, hard-*

65

ware, dry goods, clothing, millinery, bazaar goods, stoves, furniture, and building material. (They surely lived up to their slogan.)

Name Changed To Pigeon

I have been unable to find out for sure, when the name of the town was changed to Pigeon. It might have been when the Post Office was established April 21, 1890.

In the early days there were enormous flocks of wild passengers pigeons in that area so that may have been the reason that the river and town were given the name Pigeon.

These pigeons have been extinct for many years, although it has been said that their 'migration used to darken the skies.

(Pigeon Progress-Advance 11-03-1977)

Barn Raisings

As the farms were cleared there was a need for larger barns to replace the small log barns. Men went to the woods and cut logs for the timbers and lumber. Then, a 'Barn Framer' was hired to frame the barn. When he had finished this task and had all the parts laid out in proper order, a Barn Raising was held. Neighbors near and far were asked to help.

When the day arrived, two captains were chosen. They in turn picked the men for their sides. Who would have first choice? That was decided 'by lot'.

There were two men who always headed the list of those chosen. If Elias Weidman was chosen first then 'big' Ed Sturm was second or vice versa. It took strong men to left all those heavy timbers in place and fasten them securely.

There was always a race to see which side could complete their task first. With much 'Heave, Hoing' and many orders, the men worked feverishly until one side was victorious. The neighbor women helped in the house to prepare a meal for the men, which they ate when they had the barn raised.

The Pigeon Depot waiting for the Pere Marquette Train

The Pigeon Progress
(From a 1947 edition)

George H. A. Shaw

This-article was written by the Progress' first editor, whose name is unknown, in the November 11, 1897 issue.

The train was late, the merchants were influential, and so a weekly newspaper was brought to Pigeon. That's the short, short story of how the Pigeon Progress was born.

It all began in 1897 when George H. A. Shaw then of Bay City was contacted by W. F. Bernie, then publisher of the Akron newspaper. Mr. Bernie, who had an old hand made press and a quantity of type which he did not need, tried to sell the equipment to Mr. Shaw by urging him to set up a newspaper in Pigeon. Mr. Shaw a native of Tawas City was anxious to return there, but upon Mr. Bernie's insistence agreed to come to Pigeon for a look.

They arrived on the train and began their tour of the village. Mr. Shaw liked the farming section surrounding Pigeon, but he was still intent on moving to Tawas City, so he waited for the 4 p.m. train to take him to Bay City. The train was late and inquiry showed that it had been derailed between Elkton and Bad Axe. The travelers knew that it would be some time before the train would arrive, so Mr. Shaw and Mr. Bernie prepared to wait.

Meanwhile, Pigeon merchants were intrigued with the idea of a newspaper and they went to the station to try to influence Mr. Shaw to stay. Among those merchants were Henry Schluchter, Ed Bundscho, George Winter, Bill Stevens (Harness Shop) John Link (village tin-smith), and George McGillvray the station agent of the Pontiac, Oxford and Northern railroad.

The merchants were convincing and when the train finally arrived at 8 P.M., Mr. Bernie boarded it but Mr. Shaw decided to stay at least until the next day. By the next day he had decided to set up shop. His first location was upstairs in the rear in the former Fahrner Store.

There is no town along the line of the S. T. & H. Railroad from Saginaw to Bad Axe which today has better prospects than the hustling little village of Pigeon, which was sprung into existence as a natural result of the intersection of the S. T. H. and P. O. & N. Railways, at a point where both roads pass through one of the richest natural farming sections of the state. Composed, as it is, of a thrifty class of young and hustling merchants, who realize the natural advantages placed in their way and are not slow to take advantage of them. Pigeon has grown in the past three years, from a mere stopping point on these roads, to a village of about 400 inhabitants, and that growth has been of a most substantial kind. Two fine brick blocks and a brick schoolhouse, second to none in the county, grace our streets, while numerous other business blocks of frame are also to be seen. Two elevators, a planing mill and a flax mill furnish an excellent market and employment to a considerable number of hands, while there is also employment given to many others in the constant construction of new and handsome residences, of which no less than seven are at present in course of construction. There is not an empty house, nor, so far as we know, an idle man in the town, and our streets are daily crowded with farmers teams bringing to our stores and elevators the abundant products of their farms. Within the past few months alone, there have been added to Pigeon's advantage, a "newspaper, a flax mill, a new physician, (not new in practice) an addition to one of our elevators, a new dry goods and clothing house, a bakery and confectionery establishment, and our shoe shop and tin shop have undergone a complete metamorphosis and now appear as one of the largest exclusive shoe and tinware and stove emporiums, respectively, in the county. Pigeon progresses with a sound healthy growth and will continue to do' so until second to none in Huron county. It is therefore, with deepest regret, that after conducting the PROGRESS for nearly three months, we find ourselves unable, on account of ill health, to remain longer in the business here. With this issue, the 'PROGRESS changes hands and we can only say that in the change Pigeon will not, we believe, be the loser, as the new proprietor, Mr. Geo. H. A. Shaw, is like the rest of Pigeon's business men, not only a young man and a hustler, but has the necessary practical experience to enable him to make the success of the PROGRESS that its liberal patronage deserves. Again thanking the citizens of this wide awake little village for their kind and liberal treatment and patronage, we make our bow and retire. *(Pigeon Progress-Advance 11-10-1977)*

The Pigeon Progress

Those first years were a real challenge. Subscribers were few and often difficult to sell to and when they bought they usually paid for their subscriptions with produce or firewood. In those days merchants made a practice of dealing by barter and Hirshberg's store located on the ground floor under the progress office had a vast pile of wood at the rear of the store. From that wood there arose the story, told by Mr. Shaw himself, that he kept a spear and a rope in his office and that he would open the rear window, spear a chunk of Hirshberg's wood and pull it into the progress office.

The next spring Mr. Shaw moved into half of the John McLean

building, sharing it with Al Pruner "The Chicago Barber". The rent was $4.00 and payment was divided between the two.

Later, Mr. Shaw moved the Progress into what is now the office of the Pigeon Lumber Company.

In 1908 he moved his Progress into the upstairs of the Campbell Building where he remained until his sale to George V. Hartman in January of 1944. (Hartman sold to Walt Rummel in 1947 and he in turn to present owners.)

When George Shaw had been in Pigeon a short while, he met Miss Jessie Notter, the Milliner, who later became Mrs. Shaw. Jessie sold her shop to Alice Decker. (Sturm).

Music

There were very likely music teachers before my time, but my first teacher was Miss Mae McComber. The McCombers lived in the small house on west side of Brush Street, next to the railroad.

In order to take piano lessons I had to walk over three miles if I went by road to Arthur Whites, sometimes I cut across the fields.

Ida White was also taking lessons. She drove a light weight work horse named Bob, and I could ride with her to Pigeon.

A little later, Mrs. Jessie Shaw wanted piano lessons so she persuaded Miss Eleanor Biglow of Cass City to come by Pontiac, Oxford and Northern train to Pigeon and give lessons in Mrs. Shaw's home, which was where the Clinic Parking lot is today. Walter Bedford was also one of Miss Biglow's pupils. She had quite a large class. My sister, Mrs. Vera Fox, and I took lessons from her during the summers.

I still have many copies of the music magazine she recommended. It was called "The Etude".

Pigeon Baseball Team

1901 was the year the team was organized with Ed Bundescho as manager. Dr. Kaumeyeri was the pitcher, with W. A. Shriber, catcher, Jack Campbell, first base; Frank Merrick, second base; Henry

Pictured above: The baseball team of Pigeon businessmen may contain some of the men who played with the original group, but their names are not known. (*Pigeon Progress-Advance 11-17-1977*)

Schluchter, third base; George Powell, short stop; George Shaw, right field; Frank Holtzman, center field and Sol Schluchter played left field. If my memory serves me correctly, they did, not play many games.

The Fifth Factor Fertile Land

Little by little the settlers cleared their land and soon discovered that they had very fertile soil, which grew excellent crops. As already stated, there were two elevators at an early date in Pigeon. These did a larger and larger business as more land was cleared.

As is always the case: if the farmers surrounding a village are prosperous, so likewise are the merchants and farm implement dealers. Today (1977) Pigeon boasts four dealers who do a very large business.

Since the Co-Op became the sole elevator in Pigeon, it has grown immensely. In 1976, it was the second largest in the state, doing a 15 million dollar business. It employs 52 people.

School

According to a Pigeon School Annual the following have graduated. The first high school had only 10 grades, then in 1907 the eleventh grade was added and in 1909 the twelfth grade.

The first grad graduates were in 1899: Rose Sururus, Edna Sururus and Clarence Hedley. (Clarence came from the Chandler school, near Gotts Corner).In 1900, Laurence Notter, Mud Creek; Estella Lounsberry, Chandler; Joseph Maier (later Father Maier) and Kate Van Buskirk (who later taught the Hayes School in 1902-1903, and Mud Creek from 1903 to 1904. She received $33.00 a month's salary). The 1901 graduates were Henry Richmond, Mud Creek; Michael Sururus and Anna Jackson. In 1902, Gertrude Detweiler. Anna McAulay, Katie McAulay, Decker School; and Tom Schwalm were the graduating class. The graduating class of 1903 consisted of Eldon Witwer, later a successful doctor and X-ray specialist of Detroit; Harvey Schluchter, (secretary- treasurer of Ford Motor Company) and Frank Diebel a business man in Pigeon. In 1905 Flora Richmond, Russel Murdoch, both of Mud Creek graduated. In 1906, Pauline Witwer, Walter Bedford, Mud Creek; Wesley Witwer, William Baur, Mud Creek; Laurence Draher and May Schluchter graduated. In the year 1908 Katie McAulay, Fred Fox and Earnest Wilfong graduated. Fox and Wilfong were from Hayes.

At the end of the school year in 1910 the graduating class consisted of Bert Hartley and Oscar Thiel from Turner.

In a reply to my letter regarding the Pigeon school, Mary I. Schluchter stated "I started in the River School. There were two school houses on the Zimmer farm. Mr. and Mrs. Rodda were the teachers. I was in the lower grades when the Pigeon school was built. Mrs. Van Buskirk was my teacher. I also had Miss Deegan, Emily Hahn, Mrs. Wesley Wilson and then in high school Charles F. Watkins, George Bibrough and Mr. Muma. There was also Miss Keppler and Miss Brodie; Christina McAulay Cross was my first seat mate in the

River School."

The first schoolhouse in Pigeon was constructed in 1896. It cost $5,000. The lower grades were downstairs, the 7th and 8th grades on the east side of the upstairs and the high school on the west side.

The photo below shows the Pigeon school building, which burned in I916. The present building, with the exception of the north addition for the elementary grades, was it's replacement.

Pigeon High School Built in 1896 above.
This photograph shows the entire student body.

The school building was burned and then rebuilt in 1917.

In 1917 the new school was built. Later the gym and elementary buildings were added to the north of the school.

(Pigeon Progress-Advance 11-24-1977)

While the second school was being built, school had to be held in other buildings. Mrs. William Bechler wrote her eighth grade county exam in a store which at one time was Jimmie Anderson's Grocery store. At least it was near where Kretzschmer's is today. She was from the Decker school.

I have already written about the first school in Winsor township.

The first school in Mud Creek was held in the Robert Morse Sr's. log house. It was taught by Mrs. Morse.

The first Hayes (Caseville District No. 2) log school house was built in 1863. It was 14' x 18' feet in size. A bee was held to build it. There were 3 windows on each side and 2 desks the entire length of the room on each side. They were nailed to the wall, just under the windows and slanted down. In front of them were two stationary benches. There was a small platform on the east end of which stood a crude desk and chair. A rather large box stove stood in the center of the room.

The expenses for the year were $26.76. Mostly for stove, windows etc. The first term of school was June, July and August, 1863. The first teacher. was Miss Sarah Donaldson. She received. $15.00 a month, which was raised by a Rate Bill. She was paid September 2, 1863. .

At one time Turner, Winsor No. 2, Decker or Mud Creek and Hayes each had two teachers.

Consolidation

The beginning of the consolidation with Pigeon took place in 1939. "In 1939-1944 all pupils were transferred to Pigeon school from Hayes school. During 1944 Hayes consolidated with Pigeon and the school property was sold." This was also true of the other surrounding districts. Later, Elkton-Pigeon-Bay Port District was organized." Taken from "The Hayes School" written in 1965.

In the early day, when country pupils attended high school, it was quite an undertaking.

My mother walked five miles down the Sand Road to be able to attend the Caseville High School.

Later in the fall, before the school she was teaching began, she took a college subject after 4 p.m. It would be rather late before she left the school house. One night as she walked up the Sand Road a big

Country Pupils
Attend High School

bear crossed behind her. She really hurried on, then another crossed a short distance ahead and when opposite Dunn Road a mother bear and two cubs crossed in front of her. She waited until they were out of sight, then she ran the last mile home. That was the year of the "Fire of 1881".

In my day country pupils often walked 3 or 4 miles to be able to attend high school.

The Ten Cent Barn

North of the Spartan Supermarket was where the ten cent barn was situated when I went to Pigeon school. They had horses and buggies which one could hire for the day. Then, too, they would keep your horse for 10 cents a day.

When my brother Dick and I went to school in Pigeon in 1907, we drove our horse and buggy with hay for the horse in the back of the buggy, we unhitched our horse and Mr. Frank Schufelt who owned the Livery, would water the horse and give it the hay. Anna and Bert Morse did the same. In fact there were a number who did. Some rode ponies in the years that followed.

When cold weather arrived, we and the Morses rented the upstairs of Bundscho's Store. Bert worked after school hours and Saturdays for Mr. Bundscho. We had meager furnishings and brought much of the food from home.

The same year, my sister Vera Gwinn (Fox), taught the upper grades and Mona Bitchner the lower in Winsor No. 1.

Father would take the surrey, load up our belongings and supplies on Monday morning and drive to Pigeon. He then would unload us and go on to Mitchners where Vera boarded and then to the school. Friday night he reversed the trip.

In early November, I caught a bad cold and coming home on Friday night I took a heavy chill about opposite George Schubachs. Upon arriving home, I went to bed immediately with a severe case of pneumonia. There was no penicillin in those days, so the doctor didn't think I would pull through, but I made it. The case of pneumonia ended my school days for that year.

Memories Of The High School

There were two things that stand out in my memory of those days. One was our German. class. Everyone laughed when I recited. I inquired, why? They replied "You speak German like a German who speaks broken English." It's a funny thing though, through all the years I have been able to recite a German poem I learned about a forget-me-not, but I really only understand about 5 or 6 words of the eight line poem. Maybe it was lucky for me that I had to stop that course or I it would have ruined my good record.

The other thing that I remember was a large motto that Superintendent J. A. Muma had placed under the clock on the west wall. It stated, "Do It Now". Many a time I felt like putting off my studying, then I would look up at that motto and get busy. It always gave me such a feeling of satisfaction when I had finished.

Through the years, that motto has helped me over and over again. Always with the same feeling when the task was done. I have had to use that motto frequently while writing this History, for it is really quite a task, but if when it is finished it will give some enjoyment to those who read it. I shall again be satisfied!

(Pigeon Progress-Advance 12-01-1977)

Presbyterian Church

The Presbyterian church may have been built when Rev. Doremus was pastor. He later moved to Caseville.

Another pastor was Rev. Horst. Some of the families who were active in the church were: McAulays, Fosters, Brodericks, Campbells, Pauls and Spences,

Mrs. Anna Beach attended the church and sang in the choir with Marian Foster, Christine McAulay and Kate McAulay. She can't recall the names of the men who also sang with the choir.

Later, the church was discontinued and the building sold to the Masonic Lodge. It was then remodeled. after they purchased the building.

The English M. E. Church

As before stated, the church was built in 1892. It of course was a frame building. The parsonage was next, on the northeast corner of South Main and Hartley Streets. One of the early ministers was Rev. D. B. Millar. Under his pastorate the first Hayes M. E. Church was nearly completed when he was moved from Caseville to Pigeon

in 1898. Another pastor was Rev. Frank Fitchett, a young man from Pinnebog. Still another was Rev. Woodmansee whose daughters were fine musicians. Their voices added. considerably to an already fine choir. W. Horlacher was the S. S. Supt. Their W. M. S. took honors on the district one year.

Some of the names of the families who attended the church were Morrison, Schreiber, Beach, Ed Leipprandt, Heasty, Haggit, Come, Horlacher and Fox.

After some years they remodeled their church. by putting the platform on the south side of the. building instead of the east aside, and buying new circular pews to make the church more modern.

They always had a good congregation but the Detroit Conference decided it was not necessary to have two M. E. churches in one small town, so the church united with the German M. E. church. After the union of the churches, the Holiness church held services in the building for awhile, Later, it was sold and moved off the lot.

The First United Methodist Church

By 1898 the congregation had outgrown the church building in Berne. Pigeon had begun to grow while Berne declined. The debates among members who wanted to relocate in Pigeon and those who wished to remain in Berne were passionate, but the majority saw the future of the church in the young village of Pigeon, and the decision

to move was finally made.

Three lots for the location of church and parson were purchased for $170, and during the winter brick was hauled from Sebewaing and stone was hammered and wedged by hand from the Bay Port quarry.

The members of the congregation did the construction work with stone, lime and plaster. The materials were donated by the Wallace Stone Company.

(Pigeon Progress-Advance 12-07-1977)

German M. E. Church In Berne

The history of their church stated: "The congregation paid one dollar for the property on the northwest corner of Berne Road and North Caseville Road.

I had a letter from Frances C. Crawford, Wisconsin, grandson of Frances Crawford, the Lumber Baron of Caseville, provided the following information. 'While in the Register of Deeds Office looking up some information regarding some other property of his mother's, he came across the record of the Deed to the church property. Frances Crawford gave the property to the church. The $1.09 was the amount required by law.

The Deed also had a clause in it. If the property was not in use by the church, it would revert back to Frances Crawford. So Frances C. Crawford went to Ernest Clabuesch and told him, he would give the church a Quit Claim Deed. Mr. Clabuesch said it would not be necessary since the property was being used as a church cemetery.

Saint Francis Borgia Catholic Church

In 1893 a decision was made by Father Krebs and his small group of parishioners to build the first St. Francis Borgia Church. Since Pigeon was the approximate center of the villages served by Father Krebs, it was decided to build the church on the corner of Ruppert and Nitz streets where presently the old Erla's Supermarket stands. The structure, dedicated to St. Francis Borgia, was built of wood with a seating capacity of approximately 100 people.

Horseless Carriages

by Daisy LaVictoire

From the Pigeon Progress, in 1947

EDITOR'S NOTE: Longtime Pigeon resident Daisy LaVictoire has a memory few people can rival, as you'll see when you read her recollections of the earliest "horseless carriages."

On a beautiful spring day in 1905, Dr. Otto Frenzel whizzed by our farm home in his open roadster at the "break neck" speed of 10 to 15 mph., followed by billowing clouds of dust. That was my first introduction to the automobile.

About 1907, Dad (Hugh B. Harder) bought "Old Maud," an Oldsmobile with acetylene lights. The tank which produced the gas for the lights was fastened to the running board. There was no top and it had a roomy front seat. Behind it was platform with a smaller seat which could hold one large adult or three scrunched children. Dad would hold me on his lap; I put my hands on the wheel and thought I was driving.

Out for a drive in a similar car, Mr. and Mrs. E. C. Leipprandt

1912 James Spence Toy Party

sat in front, Victor (the oldest), Kenneth and Douglas (the youngest) sat in the little seat behind. The boys got in a fight and Douglas fell out. Sometime later, Mrs. Leipprandt noticed 'Douglas' absence and screamed at Vic, "Where is Douglas?" Very nonchalantly, Vic jerked his thumb back down the road saying, "He's coming back there." Doug wasn't hurt but he was very mad and dusty. Father sold our farm and we moved to my present location on Paul St. on Jan. 31, 1909.

In the winters of 1909 and 1910, Dad worked at Bad Axe selling cars for Yokon Motor Sales Co. I have a letter from his boss, whose office was in Port Huron, dated 1-17-10. The letter read as follows:

"Go to the Detroit Auto Show and get your customers to go. Push the EMF products (Everts, Maxwell and Flanders), Buick and REO. There will be a shortage of the four- cylinder REO. Yes, the Flanders '20' is a winner. Another, the roadster with a large gasoline tank in the rear which will be a big seller to the race-type driver. Go easy with the Dempt. Will be changes made in the little car

In the summers, Dad also sold farm machinery for Ernst Paul. He frequently took me with him in the buggy drawn by a roan horse named "Barney." In those days, you were invited to eat with the family

wherever you were at noon.

In the fall of 1910, father and William Heasty (of the Heasty Hotel), formed a partnership. "Heasty & Harder, Farm Implements." Besides farm implements, they sold wagons, buggies, pianos, Brush and K.R.I.T. cars. The KRIT had a top, was sleeker and more sophisticated than the Brush.

In this area, there were two traditional holiday outings -- Memorial Day, meet at the Caseville Cemetery in the morning for speeches honoring the Civil War dead and in the evening, attend a Civil War play in the Town Hall, enacted by local men.

And on July 4, the Bay Port train tracks were lined with excursion trains from Bad Axe and Saginaw, which had brought visitors from some distances. In the morning, bicycle races on the Old Bicycle Track in the park, evening ball games, speeches, etc., and a ball on occasion.

There was a city band which played in different locations and other entertainments. To top off the evening, you attended the dance in the open air pavilion.

People to whom you couldn't give a car to any other time of year, demanded one on the eve of these holidays. Away would go Dad's Demonstrator and then the family car. Fortunately there was always an old tuned-in klunker Dad could coax to life to get us to the festivities.

One gorgeous Memorial Day morning, Dad received an S.O.S from E. Hess (clothier). His Krit was stalled mid-road in front of C.F. Leipprandt's farm home. Brother Clare and I tagged along with Dad. First he looked in the gas tank under the driver seat -- it was full. Next, he checked every part of the simple motor and cranked. Then he rocked the car violently and cranked. Finally, in desperation, he gave a mighty kick to the radiator and rushed to look in the gas tank in time to see a horse fly, pop to the surface of the gasoline, jarred loose from the gas line. He plucked out the fly, cranked and voilà.

Teaching a horseman to drive could be hazardous, so Robert Haag (a liveryman) was taken way out on the back roads for his lesson. As they approached the Pinnebog River bridge, Bob froze to the wheel, yelling "Whoa! Whoa!" As they left the bridge, both men' were jarred from their seats. Fortunately, as always, the engine stalled, which was good, as Dad was laughing too hard to take control.

Courtesy of the road: when a car met a horse drawn vehicle face-to-face, the horseman jumped to his horse's head to try to calm their rearing and screaming. Usually, the horses could be coaxed and led past the car. Otherwise the automobile crawled past them.

In 1913, the partnership, Heasty & Harder dissolved and Dad built the south half of what is now McCormick's garage. The main entrance was on Main St. The office was on the south side, and near the office doom stood a gasoline pump. If the door wasn't closed, I'd sometimes pump the gasoline rather than call a mechanic, but Dad didn't think that was "ladylike."

Off and on, I was the bookkeeper. One day he asked me to fill out a car license application after they were mandatory, and I replied that I didn't know how. "Well, you can't learn any younger" and he proceeded to teach me. V. Jones was hired as a mechanic in the summer. He returned to Garber Buick's employ in the winter. When cars were bought by more people, V. Jones worked all year and moved to Pigeon. For years because of road conditions, long snows and low horse power, cars were put up on blocks in a corner off the barn, from the winter's first snowfall until roads dried up in the spring. In 1914, Father received his first contract from the Ford Motor Co. I have that contract. Before that he'd sold a variety of cars, Oaklands, Mitchells, Buicks and Studebakers.

A small Saxon roadster with a gear shift was taken in on a car deal. I knew better than to ask permission to drive it, as the shift levers were huge and clumsy -- but what a challenge from Ford Clutch drive. If I knew Dad would be out of town delivering a car, I'd hurry to the garage and get V. Jones to crank the Saxon for me, then drive down to Mile 5 Corner, praying I could get gears shifted to turn around without stalling, and get the car back in the garage in time to cool off before Dad returned.

In winter, Father took a crew of men via train to Detroit to drive new cars to Pigeon. Sometimes they drove on the ice of Lake Huron to Harbor Beach and overland home.

In summers, our whole family took the boat from Harbor Beach to Detroit and we'd drive the cars home. Heaven help you if you drove too fast or bad so the radiator boiled over -- cars were to reach Pigeon in good condition!

I doted on driving a chassis -- you felt so free sitting on a gas tank -- no wind- shield -- but always about one-third the way home, Dad ordered me to rest in a conventional car. I'd protest, "But Dad, I'm four years older than Clare, and you let HIM drive ALL the way home." "YOU ARE A GIRL! he'd say.

One day, Vera Tibbits and I had a flat tire on a water lily picking trip by Grandma Moore's bridge (owned now by Art Woelke). So what's complicated about a 30 x 3 or 30 x 31/2 tire? We changed it. Telling Dad of our achievement, he remarked resignedly, "Why do you think I hire all these men around here?" "Oh, for Women's Lib! "

Owning a gas pump was no joy either. Many a time we'd all be awakened by pounding on the door in the middle of the night by someone who'd run out of gas out in the middle of nowhere. Dad would go to the garage and, a gas can and drive the man back to his car.

In the early days, Pigeon had a Booster Club (an early Chamber of Commerce). All the businessmen who owned cars bunched up out on the street between what is now the library and Haist's Flower Shop -- filled cars with interested men, had their pictures taken, then they took off on a visit' to every town in the county.

One Sunday, they took their families all the way to Pte. Aux Barques for a chicken picnic. Such a long, hot, dusty and sandy drive.

There was special attire for these open cars. Everyone wore a tan linen duster which reached from ears to heels. Ladies wore broad brimmed, low- crowned hats, held on by a wide scarf tied under the chin so the sides could be pulled over the face to keep out dust. Men wore lightweight visored caps and "Barney Oldfield goggles."

In 1917, Dad built the north half of the garage. He installed a freight elevator and put the repair shop on the second floor. The windows were continuous on the west and north sides to give good light and ventilation. Downstairs was a large showroom, as there is now.

The first section of the garage had served as a place for a unique experience. A man with a very primitive movie machine asked to use the floor space to show his Flickers (an apt term). Dad had all the cars removed, blocks of wood were brought in and planks laid across them for seats. The operator put up a big screen at the front of the garage and we were treated to early versions of "The Perils of Pauline."

By now, Dad had tried and knew so many roads to Detroit, that Rand McNally sent a cartographer to Pigeon to have Dad draw him a map!

The first glassed-in car I recall was a 1918 Ford Sedan. What luxury from the scramble to get the side curtain out from under the backseat and buttoned on during a downpour. Side curtains also shut out the view.

Nov. 11, 1918, Father parked our Ford Sedan in front of the garage on Main St., so we could watch the first Armistice Day Parade. Brother had nearly died of influenza, and could not have watched the parade

Harder Garage was on the second floor of the auto dealership. There was a freight elevator to bring the cars up, from the first floor.

otherwise. Dad was particularly anxious for us to see this parade as World War I had been fought to end all wars.

By 1926, doctors at Ford Hospital had informed Father that he had such a serious heart condition that he could never work again. He sold the garage. (He died in 1958 at the age of 82 1/2 years).

Henry Ford, Sr. drove over from his summer home near Harbor Beach to wish him well, but admitted he hated to lose an old and trusted dealer. Dell McMann, Ford Dealer, Harbor Beach, had driven Mr. Ford to Pigeon and Dad took them to the Hotel Heasty for lunch. Mr. Heasty stood in the dining room door. Dad said "Bill, we've come for lunch." Mr. Heasty said, "My dining room is closed!" and Dad replied, "But Bill, this is Henry Ford!" Bill said in reply, "I don't give a #$#% who he is. When my dining room is closed, IT IS CLOSED!"

Mr. Ford admired that sort of stance and was so amused he laughed about it through the evening.

Albert Hartman and wife Ann Broderick Hartman - Lynn Broderick
Building on Nitz Street in 1920

News Quips From Pigeon Progress 1884 through 11/11/1901

Following are items reported in The Pigeon Progress during the period of 1883 through November of 1901. Those items of interest are presented here.

<u>1883</u> • Pontiac, Oxford, Northern Railroad passes through Berne on it's way into Caseville

<u>1884</u> • Leipprandt Bros. opened a store in Berne. In 1899 a grist mill was added.

<u>1887</u> • The Arlington House, the first hotel in Pigeon opened in 1887. Herman Kleinschmidt was the owner. (This may be inaccurate in as much as there was a Junction Hotel across from the depot which may have predated the Arlington House.)

<u>9/03/1897</u> • The Hotel Livingstone is doing a fine business. Forty people are working at the flax mills

• The bridge a mile west of Pinnebog was called the Pechette Bridge.

• Henry Diebel and Conrad Pfaff were partners in a construc tion business.

<u>9/10/1897</u> • Mrs. W. A. Schriber is named in the Schriber ad

<u>9/17/1897</u> • Hotel Livingstone formally dedicated Tuesday eve.

• School opened Monday in the new school house

• Hayes church will be dedicated a week from next Sunday

<u>10/08/1897</u> • Dr. Kaumeyer of Adrian is locating here. He will open his office next week.

<u>10/15/1897</u> • Richard Schroeder is on duty at the Arlington House

<u>10/29/1897</u> • Foundation for Dr. Frenzel's house on Main Street is complete. Diebel and Pfaff have the contract.

• G. B. Winter is proprietor of Arlington House

<u>11/04/1897</u> • Hotel Heasty is mentioned

<u>11/11/1897</u> • Corn husks wanted, cash paid — G. C. Heineman, Pigeon

<u>11/18/1897</u> • John Squan, the Indian doctor was in town yesterday.

• Geo. Farrar, manager of Hotel Heasty for past l6 mos. left.

• William Heasty, owner, took control on Monday.

<u>12/04/1897</u> • Bucket brigade to be organized. R. Schroeder, Chief.

<u>1/21/1898</u> • Dr. Fraser, Dentist of Sebewaing advertising in Prog ress

<u>1/28/1898</u> • Dr. Scott residence to be moved from Berne by Diebel and Pfaff.

• New grist mill will be built by Diebel and Pfaff

<u>2/18/1898</u> The new school at Bay Port is ready for use.

<u>3/04/1898</u> • Winsor F. & A. M. hall dedicated and officers installed by F. O. Gilbert. G. M., of Bay City

<u>3/11/1898</u> • Old school house moved to town by Diebel and Pfaff, will be used as a store.

<u>3/l8/1898</u> • P. O.&.N. bridge north of town damaged by high water, could not be crossed.

• Ada Lobdell opened a millinery next to Schluchter store

• Albert Kleinschmidt appointed postmaster on March l5, 1898

<u>3/25/1898</u> • Presbyterian services in Pigeon in the morning, in Hayes in the afternoon and in Caseville in the evening to be conducted by Rev. Ross.

• E. B. Clark was one time proprietor of Bay Port Hotel.

<u>4/29/1898</u> • Freeland photography studio move to Pigeon from Elkton.

• Leinbach house on Charles Street built

• C. F. Watkins of Metamora engaged to be in charge of school.

• Dressmaking by Nina and Sarah McDonald — over the Schluchter store

• Advertisements — Foster and Challis, machinery; Dan Fisher, blacksmith; Leyrer & Eimers, meat market; Louis Staubus, wheels (bicycles): Sol Schluchter; John McLean, plows; Ada Lobdell: , Jessie Notter; E. F. Hess: Jos. Schluchter, A. Hirsch berg, G. C. Heineman, Farmer's Bank, F. E. Holtzman, tailor.

<u>7/08/1898</u> H. C. Wideman, meat market

<u>8/05/1898</u> • Pigeon now has a band.

  • Ernst Paul is manager of flax mill

<u>8/26/1898</u> • Telephone lines from Bay Port to Pigeon have been contracted.

<u>9/02/1898</u> • Valentine Heck purchased an Empire drill this week.

<u>9/09/1898</u> • Sugar factory in Bay City is the first in the state.

  • F. W. Neusis called to Berne school — accepted 80 scholars.

<u>9/16/1898</u> • Fred Copeland, clerk at Heasty House, left. B. Tahash took over.

<u>9/23/1898</u> • Wesley Sedibarton farewell sermon at Presbyterian church after three months.

<u>10/29/1898</u> • Road from Berne to Pigeon on east side of P. O.&.N. tracks being built.

<u>12/02/1898</u> • Talk of moving Evangelical church to Pigeon from Berne.

<u>12/16/1898</u> • Arlington Hotel now lighted by acetylene gas.

<u>1/13/1899</u> • Well, what are we going to do about the sugar factory?

<u>1/20/1899</u> • Wallace shipped carloads of beets from Bay Port to Bay City — 17% sugar — largest % sent to plant.

  • Revival meetings are being held in the Presbyterian church at this place.

<u>1/27/1899</u> • Hotel Hannah now lighted by electricity.

  • It was decided at a meeting of the members of the Evangelical church at Berne this evening to move the church to Pigeon.

  • Plans for the new German Methodist Church are finished.

<u>2/03/1899</u> • Sand for the new German Methodist Church is about to be hauled.

<u>2/10/1899</u> • Caro will have a sugar factory.

<u>2/07/1899</u> • Brick is on the ground for John McLean's new store.

  • Caseville says they will have a sugar factory or go bust.

<u>2/24/1899</u> • 24th of February and no sleighing yet.

  • Henry Diebel contracted for moving Evangelical church

<u>3/03/1899</u> • Sure thing — Elkton and Bad Axe will not have a

sugar factory this year.

• During the Holidays, work commenced on moving Evangelcal church, and a 26 x 36 addition to Winsor No. 1 School (Winsor School) was started by Wellington Horlacher, contractor.

3/03/1899 • Until Evangelical church is moved and ready for occupancy, services will be held in the Presbyterian church at 2:00 every Sunday afternoon.

3/17/1899 • John Diebel purchased the shingle mills at Wolfton

• Timber is being cut for the new German Methodist Church

3/24/1899 • Sand and stone for Evangelical church hauled this week

3/21/1899 • The l4 dwelling houses that were moved from Sebewaing to the Bay Port quarries have all been placed.

4/07/1899 • Infant child of James Smith of Mud Creek died Sunday, buried Tuesday.

4/21/1899 • Work will be commenced on the foundation of the new German Methodist Church about May lst.

5/05/1899 • Mrs. Carrie Ives Saunders is the new manager of the Bay Port Hotel.

• Well drilled on the German Methodist premises this week.

• Samuel Goodwell, manager of the Grassmere Stock Farm will plant 800 apple trees on the farm this spring . The trees were purchased from the nursery of Geo. W. Lewis of Monroe.

5/26/1899, • Carpenters are at work finishing Dr. Frenzel's new home.

• Leipprandt Bros. getting material on ground for two story resience, Block 9, Lot ll, Main Street

• German Methodist Church traded an acre and a half on end of Mabel St. for Lots 39, 40, 41 on Michigan Ave. belonging to Mose Gregory.

6/02/1899 • German Methodist Episcopal church sold parsonage at Berne to Robert Stortz. Will commence erection of new parsonage on church premises soon.

6/23/1899 • Grand opening of new Hotel Heasty has been set for next Saturday, July l.

• W. J. Stevens sold building and business to Fred Clabuesch.

7/21/1899 • Work on new addition to Arlington House being pushed

• Contract for Hirshbergs new store let to Zimmer and Bowman of Sebewaing — 91' x 31' — 2 story — brick.

8/04/1899 • Two hotels in town - Heasty and Arlington.

• Hotel rooms being added above McLean's store

• Buffalo Bill will be at Bay City August 10th

8/18/1899 • German M. E. parsonage ready for shingling

• John McLean and Lizzie Rather married.

9/08/1899 • Pews for German M. E. church arrived.

10/06/1899 • Balcony being erected at Hotel Heasty and McLean's Bldg

• Businessmen met to discuss change in town's name.

10/13/1899 • Work is being done on the steeple of the new German M. E. church.

• Dan Fisher leases blacksmith business to James Kline of Elkton to devote more time to dray business.

10/27/1899 • Bridge on Broderick road called Samuel Foster bridge.

11/10/1899 • Infant child of Mr. and Mrs. J. W. Leipprandt was the first christened in the new German M. E. church.

11/17/1899 • Sebewaing is now talking sugar factory. It is claimed that from $150,000 to $200,000 of home money can be raised.

11/24/1899 • Scheffer and Snyder — City Laundry.

12/01/1899 • Dr. Kaumeyer married Fafa Schluchter of Kilmanagh.

12/08/1899 • G. H. A. Shaw and Jessie Notter married at home of her parents in Caseville on Wednesday.

1/02/1900 • Two elevators and one grist mill in town.

2/16/1900 • The Free Will Baptists are getting the material on the ground for a new stone church at Snell's Corner.

5/18/1900 • G. E. Mcillmurry is teaching at the Tarry School

6/08/1900 • Work is being rushed on E.W.E. Bundscho's new residence on South Main Street. (Robert Tate Home).

6/15/1900 • The German Lutherans of Saginaw will run an excursion to the village next Sunday, and a meeting will be held at the river flats south of town.

7/06/1900 • Schriber building — 32' x 70' — 2 story brick

10/26/1900 • P. O.&N. bridge south of town undergoing repairs.

11/02/1900 • The Caseville grist mill receiving considerable repairs and expects to be in operating in a short time. W. E. Lutz, formerly of Pigeon, will have charge.

11/30/1900 • Pigeon Lutheran church society are building a fine shed for the use of teams.

11/08/1901 • Leipprandt Bros. received contract to furnish all lumber for the Mitchner church to be built one mile south of the old town hall.

8/02/1901 • The fine brick farm resident of William Bainer (Boehner) just west of town is rapidly nearing completion.

9/20/1901 • The school was closed yesterday on account of the funeral of our late President McKinley.

10/02/1901 • The ground was broken last week for the Sebewaing Sugar Factory.

10/04/1901 • Chris Schuette and Sophie Bergman married.

10/11/1901 • Architect C. L. Cowles of Saginaw has a cottage on Bay Port shores. He was the architect for the buggy factory and designed a new masonic hall that was never built.

Population of Huron County

Following is the population of Huron county according to United States census reports beginning with the census of 1850.

1850	210	1900	34,162
1860	3,165	1910	34,758
1870	9,040	1920	32,786
1880	20,089	1930	31,132
1890	28,545	1940	32,584

Plowing with the force of six men

This 8-bottom plow, with 4 men operating the plow-depths, is pulled by a steam engine. Apparently there wasn't much worry about soil compaction in those days, but perhaps there was so much humus in the ground that soil drainage was no problem. With this much demand for manpower on a plowing operation, it's obvious why farmers weren't able to handle more than 60 or 80 acres. Steam engines were in their heydays between the 1890's and 1920's

Section Crew In 1897

The above photograph was taken at the time Pigeon Elevator (Wallace and Orr Company, of Bay Port) was being built. One of the men in the picture is Fred Block, father of William Block of Caro.
(From Pigeon Progress 1947)

Pigeon In The 1890s

From The Pigeon Progress dated 1947

In 1898 the John Diebel addition was platted and the large Hirshberg store was built. Previously Hirshberg's were in the store now known as the Louis Staubus building. Mr. Staubus purchased the building from Geo. B. Winter.

The Berne flax mill was destroyed by fire and was rebuilt by Henry C. Weidman on the site now occupied by Norman Schaaf's tile works, in 1896. Ernst Paul was manager. The mill was operated by James Livingston &. Co. Succeeding Mr. Paul, James Bright was manager for a few years, Carl Stoner also managed the mill for a time.

John J. Campbell came to Pigeon in 1896 and purchased a small drug store which had been operated a short time. He was then located in a small one-story building located where the Buerker barber shop is now.

William Stevens was the harness maker and he was located in a two story frame building where the Greene grocery store is now.

The Farmer's Bank building was next to the Schriber building on the north.

JOHN J. CAMPBELL,

DEMOCRATIC CANDIDATE
FOR REPRESENTATIVE
TO THE STATE LEGISLATURE.

H. H. Gould conducted an implement business in what is now Doepker's store.

Gotleib Glosser had his Saloon in the building now occupied by Spence Bros. Gotleib did not have a cash register. Change was kept neatly arranged on the back bar. If he had occasion to step out and leave the place in charge of the bartender, he always counted the money before he went out and again when he came back. If a customer "ran his face" he would charge it with chalk on the glass of the back bar. It is needless to say the amounts never were very large.

Jessie N. Notter conducted a millinery store in a small building where the A & P store is now, and John Moore had a restaurant on the present side of Orr's drug store.

A little one story building on the present site of the People's Oil & Gas Co. was the home of the Progress and Pruner's barber shop.

Frank Mehnifik and Harry Gould sported fast horses and on two or three occasions they had contests down Main street. We don't remember which one had the fastest horse.

There had been no bar in the then Hotel Heastv until it was taken over by Leughlin & Powell.

Those days Main St. south turned east at the corner opposite the Cross Lutheran church and ran along the railroad track to the main road south of Pigeon.

There were only thirty-five dwelling houses in Pigeon Village fifty years ago.

When the Ford (Model T) came on the market, it was priced at $950.

There were no homes in the Gould addition, five or six east of the P. O.& N. Railway. About 12 or 15 in the Nitz addition and about 8 or 10 in the Moeller addition.

No cement sidewalks were built until after the village was incorporated in 1903.

Business and Professional Men 1882 - 1909

Pigeon Progress -1974

By Gerard Schultz

In 1882, the tracks of the Pontiac, Oxford and Northern Railroad were laid across Winsor Township. The station between Kilkenny and Caseville was named Berne. Kilkenny is now known as Linkville. In 1886, the Saginaw, Tuscola and Huron Railroad flung its track across the northern bound railroad. The crossing of the two railroads marked the real beginning of the present Village of Pigeon. This crossing of the two railroads was first called Berne Junction.

Because of the existence of Berne, the establishment of the Pigeon post office was delayed until April 20, 1890. As early as 1886, all passenger trains made regular stops at Berne Junction. It may be of interest that at the time of the establishment of a post office at Pigeon, there were 36 other post offices in Huron County. Only a few years later, many of these post offices were discontinued because of the establishment of Rural Free Delivery.

Sixty-five years ago, Albert Kleinschmidt was postmaster at Pigeon, having held the position since the time of the establishment of the post office. Edwin C. and]ohn W. Leipprandt, known as the Leipprandt Bros., operated a general store, sold farm implements, owned a grain elevator, which specialized in navy beans and seeds. They also owned the Pigeon Milling Company.

George H. A. Shaw was editor and publisher of the Pigeon Progress. F. W. Merrick was cashier of the Farmers Bank of Frank W. Hubbard, Ernest Clabuesch was cashier of the Pigeon State Bank. The agent of the American Express Company was Frank F. Downer. McElmurray and Elenbaum were proprietors of the Arlington Hotel. Edmund Bundscho sold hardware. John J. Campbell was druggist, jeweler and local manager of the Valley Telephone Company. E. T. Leipprandt operated the McKinley Township Farmers Telephone line.

Daniel Fisher, Fred Gotthardt and Robert Haggett still derived their livelihood from blacksmithing. Fisher was a blacksmith for many years. Perry L. Fritz was dentist. Walter B. Freeland made his living as a photographer. Frank Sheufelt maintained a livery. He

Shown here are Eddie, Beatrice and Daniel Fisher, their father, in front of the Fisher Blacksmith Shop.

had horses and buggies for rent and stabled horses. John McLean sold hardware, groceries and was manager of the Michigan State Telephone Company. Hugh B. Harder was prominent in farming and business. Ralph E. Dawson, Qtto Frenzel and Wm. T. Morrison were physicians. James Bright managed the Flax Company, which was located on the present site of the tile plant. Flax was a cash crop for farmers.

Rev. Floyd R. Harding was minister of the Methodist Episcopal Church, Rev. Theodore Hey was pastor of the German Methodist Episcopal Church, and Rev. Charles Rodesiler was pastor of the Evangelical. Church. Other churches were a Catholic Church, a Lutheran Church and a Presbyterian Church.

John A. McLean also managed the Huron County Creamery. Walter W. Loosemore was butcher. Donald C. McDonald sold and delivered coal. Ernest Paul sold agricultural implements. Frank Kinch was manager of the Pigeon Butter Company. Theodore Wills was in charge of the Pigeon Cold Storage Company. H. Schultz was the man to see at the Pigeon Elevator Company. Hartley and Horlacher of the Pigeon Planing Mill sold building supplies.

Alfred H. Sauer was a lawyer. George H. Schnell was plumber and sold hardware. Wm. A. Schriber represented a very common combination of furniture and undertaking. Eustus Schwalm cut hair, shaved and trimmed beards. Mrs. Jessie Shaw was milliner. Thomas

O. Shaw was a grocer. Clarence , A. Shoemaker represented the Pere Marquette Railroad and. the U. S. Express Company.

Daniel McAulay was agent for the Standard Oil Company. Louis Stabus sold boots and shoes. Thomas and Lovina Thiel sold groceries and dry goods. Fred M. Warner had a cheese factory. Fred Clabuesch and Samuel Witwer were harness-makers. Mrs. J. H. Woolley supplied women with dresses, hats, bonnets and ribbons.

In 1909, the estimated population of Pigeon was 700.

A thank you to Mr and Mrs. E. T. Leipprandt.

Pigeon Businesses

From 1904 Huron County Plat Book

Bundscho & Heasty

Dealers in Heavy and Shelf Hardware, Builders' Hardware, Coal and Wood Stoves, Kitchen Utensils, Tinware, Paints, Nails, 'Wire, etc. Wagons, Buggies, Farming Implements, etc.

Diebel & Giese

Dealers in General Merchandise. A full line of Dry Goods, Groceries, Clothing, Ladies' and Gents Furnishings, Hats, Caps and Shoes, etc.

Diebel, John

Manufacturer of and Dealer in Pine, Hemlock and Hardwood Lumber. Lath. Shingles, and all kinds of House Finishing Materials. Cistern and Stock Tanks a specialty. Mill and Threshing Supplies. Belting, Oil and Steam Fittings. Manufacturer of Concrete Building Blocks, the cheapest and best building material on earth.

Farmers' Bank of Pigeon.

F. W. Merrick, Cashier. A general banking business transacted. Loans made, etc. .

Parrar, George B.

Prop. of Hotel Heasty. First-class hotel. Rates, $2.00 per day. Special attention to our table. Bar in connection.

Frenzel, Otto

Physician. Calls promptly answered.

Gould, R. I.

Dealer in Buggies, Wagons. and all kinds of Farm Implements. Cream Separators, etc.

Hartley, Albert

Manager of the Pigeon Planing Mill. Dealer in Lumber Lath Shingles etc.

Hirschberg, A. & Son

Dealers in General Merchandise. A full line of Shoes, Cloaks, Carpets, Groceries, Hardware, Dry Goods, Clothing. Millinery, Bazaar Goods, Stoves, Furniture and Building Material.

Kaumeyer, A. G.

Physician and Surgeon. Office at residence north of Hirschberg's store. Calls promptly answered. '

Leipprandt Brothers

Dealers in General Merchandise. Grain and Produce Buyers and Dealers. A full and complete line of Dry Good, Ladies' and Gents' Furnishing Goods, Clothing, Shoes, Groceries. etc.

Loosemore, W. W.

Prop. of the City Meat Market. Dealer in all kinds of Fresh and Salt Meat, etc. Buyer and Shipper of Live Stock, Dressed Hogs and Poultry, etc;

McElmurray & Elenbaum.

Props. of the Arlington House. Rates $1 to $1.50 per day. We make a specialty of catering to the traveling trade. Livery in connection. Sample room and good bar in connection. Wholesale distributors of the famous Elchardt &. Becker Beer.

McLean, John A.

Dealer in General Hardware. Tin shop in connection. Eaves Troughing a specialty. Warm Air and Steam Heating Plants installed. Wind Mills and Power Machinery.

Powell, George O.

Dealer in Fine Wines, Liquors and Cigars. Fresh Beer always on tap

Shaw. Geo. E. A.

Publisher and Editor of the Pigeon Progress. Published every Friday. Job Printing neatly executed.

Shuefelt, Frank

Livery, Sale and Feed Stable. First-class turn-outs. Rates reasonable. Special attention to the traveling public.

J. W. Leipprandt celebrating his 90th birthday on September 11, 1947

Land Where Pigeon Is Located Traded for Shotgun

The Pigeon Progress from Sept. 26,1947

There were no hard surface, roads in the county and only a very few miles of gravel that were poorly built.

That reminds us! The first automobile to arrive in Pigeon was driven by Frank W. Hubbard, a French make. Later, for a number of years, it was news for the local paper when anyone sported a new gasoline wagon.

In Huron county towns only the best hotels charged a dollar for a bed, and they served meals from 25 cents, that included meat, potatoes, two or three side dishes and a large piece of pie.

The girl who had a beau who sported a nice speedy driver and a rubber tired buggy was the envy of half the other girls in the community.

Bay Port entertained Sunday excursions. Sometimes as many as four or five trains.

School children walked to and from school. Many cases as far as three and four miles.

School teachers in the grades were paid $35 and $40 a month. The superintendent of the Pigeon school received the princely sum of $900 a year.

After the frost went out in the spring, the mud on Main Street in Pigeon was two-thirds up to the hub of the wagon and roads out in the country were no better. It took a good team to haul a 500 pound load and even then it was necessary to rest the team every quarter mile.

If a woman wore dresses so short that you could see her ankle, she was talked about.

When the S. T. &,H. Railroad. crossed the P. O. & N., what is now Pigeon was called Berne Junction.

John Adams was the first President of the United States to occupy the White House, into which he moved in 1800.

Pigeon is now located where seventy or eighty years ago there was nothing but marsh land.

In 1883 there was one building which was located just south of the present depot across the Pere Marquette track. It was torn down about 12 years ago. About 1881 there was also the farm home of Henry Moeller, Sr. and it was located where the former Charles Witwer cheese factory stood. Another was a little building just east of the home now occupied by Harry Haist. It was erected by John Glosser, an old river driver on the Pigeon river, who owned the forty acres which, is now Main Street and south of Michigan Ave. One story is, that he traded the property for a shotgun and he is reported to have said that while the shotgun wasn't worth a dam, the fellow, he made the trade with was stung.

When the tracks of the Pontiac, Oxford and Northern Railroads were first laid through this section in 1882 there was little belief that a town would ever be built at this point because of the fact that the town of Berne only lay one mile to the north. The coming of the Saginaw, Tuscola & Huron Railroad down through this section in 1886, however, changed the plans and ideas and there were those who believed that the intersection of the two railroads would be a desirable location for a town. Charles Applegate, the first station agent in Pigeon, induced John Nitz, a farmer living south of Pigeon, to plat what is now known as the Nitz & Applegate addition. He erected the first store building in Pigeon, and carried a small stock of merchandise. This was in 1887. He then sold the building, which was located where the Gulf (up-town gas station) is now, to Leipprandt Bros, of Berne, who opened up a branch store. In 1881 Joseph Schluchter, who was also in Berne, opened up a branch store in a building located about where Schumacher's meat market is now.

Among the early buildings was the Arlington Hotel, erected by Herman Kleinschmidt. Later in 1889 the hotel was sold to George Winter, who conducted the hotel for a number of years until he sold out to Robert McElmurray and Lee Elenbaum.

In 1889 Herman and Albert Kleinschmidt purchased the Schluchter building and put in a line of general merchandise. It was in 1888 that John Diebel built his saw mill, the union depot was built, and George F. McNiel erected a building and operated a store where the Gem Theater was later located. In 1889 C. C. Heineman, purchased the building and for about six years conducted a furniture and undertaking business. About this time William Goff opened up the first harness shop in Pigeon on the location of the building now occupied by Lyman Gregory's furniture store.

The post office was located in Pigeon in 1888 with Albert Kleinschmidt as postmaster, which he held with the exception of four years during Cleveland's second administration, when his brother Herman was the postmaster for four years, until George Anklam was appointed under president Wilson's first administration.

The first church, the Catholic, was erected in 1889, on the lot now occupied by Maust's Super Market. The English M. E. and Presbyterian churches were built in 1892, The Masonic Temple is now on the location of the Presbyterian church.

In 1891 a creamery was erected but was destroyed by fire a year later. And for a few years later Charles Wittwer ran a Swiss cheese factory

In 1890 Pigeon which up to that time had. been slow in growth, took a new lease of life, and from that time until the present, development and advancement has been apparent each year.

In 1890 Liken & Bach of Sebewaing purchased the John Diebel saw mill and converted it into a stave and heading plant which they operated until 1890 on the site of the present Pigeon Lumber Co. After disposing of his saw mill, Mr. Diebel built his planing mill in 1890 on the present site of the Diebel Auto Co. Sometime later the plant was destroyed by fire, but was subsequently rebuilt and for a number of years was conducted by Charles Prast until after the second fire.

In 1895 Joseph Schluchter and Leipprandt Bros. moved their interests to Pigeon, and later that year, Leipprandt erected a grain elevator. The S. T. & H. Railroad Company also built an elevator about the same time. It was in 1895, also, that Wallace & Orr Co., of Bay Port, erected a building and put in a stock of general merchandise. One year later they sold the store and property to Joseph Schluchter. This building occupied the site of the present building owned by J. W. Leipprandt & Son.

In 1895 Henry Moeller Sr. platted what is now known as (the north end of town The Crawford Estate plat was also recorded about the same time. The Maccabee hall was also erected about the same time. The same building is now used as a hardware store by John Diebel. The Hotel Heasty was also built in 1895 by William Heasty and John A. McLean. McLean ran a grocery and hardware whre the Hotel Vollmer bar room is now located. The third floor addition, on the west of the hotel, was erected in 1914. Following Mr. Heasty, those who conducted the hotel in the early days were George S. Farrar, O. M. Brooks, Laughlin & Bowell, Geo. C. Powell and Charles Schneck.

Frank Hubbard & Co. established the Farmer's Bank in 1895 which was the first bank. F. W. Merrick was the cashier. In 1906 Arnott & Marks of Sanilac county opened up the Pigeon State Bank which was absorbed by Hubbard interests in 1908.

The first Pigeon school was erected in 1896 at a cost of $5,000. In I916 the building was destroyed by fire and the present building completed the following year. Eleven years ago the high school gym was erected.

Putting A Face To The Name

A. G. Kaumeyer

Albert Hartley

H. H. Gould

Harry Hirshberg

Joseph Schluchter
President

E.W.E. Bundscho
Clerk

Louis Staubus

J. W. Leipprandt

The People Of Pigeon At Work!
Information From
The Pigeon Diamond Jubilee Book

Clabuesch's Harness Shop was a very busy place until the automobile caught on. Trunks and buggy whips are pictured in the window of what was later Polewach's store, and is now Thumb Cellular's building. From left to right are Waldemar Rupp, Samuel Witwer, Frederick Clabuesch and his sons Raymond and Walter. The time is estimated at the early 1920's.

Hiring out as a clerk in one of the Village's many hustling new businesses was yet another way to put bacon on the table. Pictured are some of the employees at Hirshberg's.

Art Smith, manager of Warner's Creamery, is pictured. He and his bride, Louise Diebel, lived upstairs over the creamery, which was located on North Main Street. Butter and even cheese were made from whatever cream could be purchased from the farmers.

"Workin' on the Railroad" was more than a song for many early Pigeon settlers. Pictured from left to right are Henry LaFond, Peter Anderson, Ed Danks, Wes Schafer, George Klinger, John Danks, George Walsh and Tom Lockhart.

NOTES

NOTES

NOTES

Made in the USA
Columbia, SC
23 August 2023

21906280R00065